William Lloyd Garrison
and the
Humanitarian Reformers

The Library of American Biography

EDITED BY OSCAR HANDLIN

Russel B. Nye

William Lloyd Garrison

and the

Humanitarian Reformers

Edited by Oscar Handlin

Little, Brown and Company • *Boston* • *Toronto*

Published simultaneously in Canada
by Little, Brown & Company (Canada) Limited

PRINTED IN THE UNITED STATES OF AMERICA

Editor's Preface

ALMOST all Americans agreed in 1800 that slavery was a dying institution. Even in the South it seemed clear this form of servitude would soon disappear. Yet two decades later slavery had once again become a fixed feature of the economic and social order. Before long its continued existence formed a great moral issue that divided the nation and led it into civil war. The extension of cotton culture and the growth of manufacturing gave new vitality to Negro bondage so that it was not to vanish of itself but would either survive or be extirpated.

Slavery thus challenged the mounting tide of reform sentiment that spread through the United States after 1820. Increasingly, earnest men and women began to devote their lives to the suppression of the intolerable evil of human slavery. The abolition movement grew steadily, and in good part derived its strength from its position in the more general reform movement. This was but the brightest star in a great galaxy of causes by which Americans of the nineteenth century hoped to advance the condition of mankind.

Behind all these excited endeavors was the conviction that men had the power to transform the universe in accord with their moral ideals. Just as they had been capable of conquering a wilderness, of extending civilization to the most savage ends of the earth, so too they thought themselves capable of reforming inherited traditions and institutions to improve and ameliorate the condition of humanity. The Americans were confident that evil, though often present in man, was not inherent in his character, and was to be eliminated in a proper social order.

The certainty that reform was possible was nurtured by the faith that man played a role in a great drama of progress that was leading him to ultimate perfectability. All evil had its source not in man's nature, but in corruptions from without. Progress demanded only that the corrupting elements be removed by reforms — abolition, universal education, temperance, and the host of others that absorbed the energies of Americans between 1820 and 1860. These convictions agitated a good part of American society in those excited decades.

William Lloyd Garrison was intimately associated with all these developments. His name became synonymous, in time, with the abolitionist cause. Yet his interests were not narrowly confined to that movement. Rather, his life graphically and dramatically illustrated the complexity of the reform impulse as a whole, and his career touched upon a variety of issues that came to a head in those years. In Russel B. Nye's lucid account, the man himself stands forth clearly in his strength and weakness; and through the man we perceive the nature of the very significant movements in which he was closely involved.

OSCAR HANDLIN

Contents

William Lloyd Garrison
and the
Humanitarian Reformers

For
Pete

Prologue

THE AMERICAN of the early nineteenth century faced the future with magnificent self-assurance. "There is at hand," remarked William Ellery Channing in 1830, "a tendency and a power to exalt the people," founded on "devotion to the progress of the whole human race." So too the Shaker seeress, Paulina Bates, welcomed "the present age as commencing the most extraordinary and momentous era that ever took place on earth." The men of Emerson's and Jackson's time looked ahead toward a better society, a perfected democracy, an inspiring future. In this spirit of confidence, compounded of idealism, liberalism, humanitarianism, and democracy, Americans sought to reform, repair, and redirect their society.

Nineteenth-century reform was not an evangelism of the underprivileged, or a class bootstrap-lifting of the oppressed, but a movement in which rich and poor, cultured and uneducated, radical and conservative, joined alike. Neither was it a mass religious revival, like the Great Awakening a century before. It was a planned, rational, pragmatic effort (with the eccentric, it is true, showing at the edges) to realize for once and all the innate capabilities of mankind.

The wise man in Concord put his finger on its central principle. "What is a man born for," asked Emerson, "but to be a Reformer, a Remaker of what man has made?" This conviction sent hardheaded Yankee workmen into utopian communities; it sent cultured gentlewomen poking into jails and madhouses; it sent Unitarian ministers and practical politicians into the hurly-burly of abolitionism. They all trusted the individual and believed in his ability to improve himself and the world he had made. They all labored hard, each in his way, to remove impediments from his path. A good digestion, a ten-hour working day, sensible clothing and rights for women, temperance, better jails, labor unions, utopian economics, and a state of spiritual communion with God were each of them steps that might advance humanity a few paces nearer the ideal society.

With political equality apparently achieved, and the hold of an old authoritarian theology apparently broken, the nation in 1830, therefore, turned its attention to the problem of making American society perfect. There were many reforms and reformers, but, as James Russell Lowell noted, there was in them all "a very solid and serious kernel, full of the most deadly explosiveness. It was simply a struggle for fresh air . . . this life that the reformers demanded." Harriet Martineau, completing her tour of the United States in 1836, remarked that she found there "a remarkable set of people living and acting vigorously in the world, with a well-grounded faith, directed toward a noble object" — that of creating a better world.

William Lloyd Garrison was one of these reformers.

I

My Name Shall Be Known

EXACTLY WHEN Joseph Garrison arrived in Nova Scotia (the old name for New Brunswick) the records do not show. An Englishman, probably of distant French origin, Joseph may have paused first in Massachusetts before moving north, where land grants along the St. John River attracted settlers from New England in the mid-eighteenth century. At any rate, when a group of settlers arrived from Essex County, Massachusetts, in the spring of 1763, Joseph Garrison was already there. A year later he married Mary Palmer, daughter of Daniel, descended from solid old Massachusetts stock of Hunts, Wheelers, Palmers, and Stickneys. When Tract 109 of Sunbury County opened in 1765, Joseph was granted four hundred acres of bottom land that he farmed for the rest of his life. Mary bore him nine children, one of whom was Abijah, born in 1773. Joseph died ten years later, but Mary lived until 1822, hearty, energetic, and a thoroughgoing Baptist to the last.

Abijah Garrison, who did not like farming, chose to follow the sea. He was a tall, fair, handsome man, his good looks marred by a birthmark across his throat from ear to ear. A skillful and conscientious seaman, he became a

sailing master while still quite young. On a trip to
Deer Island, near Passamaquoddy, he met Frances Maria
Lloyd, whose father, Andrew, worked as a pilot in
Quoddy waters. Fanny, a tall, strong girl, was a Baptist
convert who lived with her uncle, since her father, a devout Episcopalian, had disowned her. Abijah was attracted to her at once, and after a brief and highly formal
courtship, they were married in 1799. They lived in St.
John, N. S. (where they lost their first child) until 1801,
moving to Granville about 1803, where James Holley and
Caroline Eliza were born. But Abijah found sailing berths
in Nova Scotia harder and harder to get, until, "disaffected toward the government" and "tired of the barren-
ness of these Eastern climates," he decided to move to
Massachusetts. Newburyport, Massachusetts's third city in
size and a port of some importance, seemed a likely place
to settle. Abijah and Fanny found rooms on School Street
with another seaman, Captain Farnham, where shortly
after their arrival, on December 12, 1805, William Lloyd
Garrison was born. Mrs. Farnham, also a devout Baptist,
helped Fanny with the children, attended church with her,
and became her close friend.

At first there were plenty of jobs for a good sailing
master, but Abijah Garrison's luck failed to hold. The Embargo of 1807 slowly throttled New England's sea trade
and left Newburyport's wharves deserted, and Abijah
spent more and more time at local taverns with his sailing
cronies. He was not a habitual drinker, but enforced idle-
ness, added to a crowded house filled with prayer meetings
and tumbling infants, proved to be more than he could
bear. Caroline died in 1808, a few weeks before Fanny
gave birth to another daughter, Maria Elizabeth. Abijah

drowned his sorrows, came home tipsy, and had a scene
with his wife. A month later he left Newburyport for
good. Traces of him were found in New Brunswick as late
as 1814, but the date and place of his death are unknown.
None of his children had any clear memory of him, except that he was "a kind, genial man." Fanny Garrison
rarely spoke of him again.

Newburyport suffered during the Embargo years, and
there was little steady work for a woman with three small
children. Mrs. Farnham charged the abandoned family
only nominal rent. (For food the Garrisons occasionally
had to beg. One of William Lloyd's earliest memories was
his trip with a tin pail to the houses on High Street, where
he collected leftovers from the tables of the wealthy.) He
was slow in school, lefthanded (almost a sin to nineteenth-century schoolmasters) and shy with schoolmates.
Fanny found irregular jobs as a domestic or nurse, but
she was never more than a few days away from public
charity. James and Lloyd worked at odd jobs, running er-
rands, helping with chores, selling homemade molasses
candy in the streets on court or market days. But even
Fanny Garrison's iron determination could not keep her
family together; there was too little work, and too little
to eat. In 1812 she moved to Lynn with her eldest son
James, who took an apprenticeship in a shoe factory. The
infant Maria stayed with the Farnhams, while seven-year-
old Lloyd went to live with Ezekiel Bartlett, a Baptist
deacon who had two daughters and needed a boy for
chores.

Young Lloyd attended school sporadically and worked
hard for Bartlett. The Bartletts liked the boy and were
kind to him, sent him to Baptist church regularly, and en-

couraged him to sing in the choir. For nearly two years he lived a fairly normal boyhood life, until in 1814 his mother brought him to Lynn and apprenticed him to a Quaker shoemaker. It was hard and confining work for a boy of nine; the thread cut his fingers, and he remembered for years how his legs ached from holding the heavy lapstone. Fanny Garrison, with James and Lloyd with her, hoped soon to bring her daughter to Lynn. But in 1815 a shoe manufacturer named Newhall announced the opening of a branch factory in Baltimore and advertised for labor. Fanny and her boys joined the group of workmen bound for Baltimore, arriving in October, 1815.

The shoe factory never opened. Newhall gave the Garrison family rooms for a time, while Fanny did housework and nursing. James worked in a shoeshop, and Lloyd swept floors, but after Newhall returned to Lynn Fanny found work scarce. Young James, unhappy and rootless, ran away to sea, to be heard from only infrequently for years. Lloyd, too, was lonesome — so discontented, Fanny wrote Mrs. Farnham, "he would leave me tomorrow and go with strangers to N.D. (Newburyport); he can't mention any of you without tears." Nor could Fanny make enough at nursing to support him; regretfully she sent him back to Deacon Bartlett, where he stayed for slightly more than a year. Then, believing the boy should learn a trade, Bartlett apprenticed him to a Haverhill cabinet-maker, Moses Short. Short was a kind master, but the lonely boy ran away within six weeks. Short recaptured him near Newburyport, and, realizing that the youngster was desperately unhappy, released him from his apprenticeship and sent him back to Deacon Bartlett's, the only real home the boy had ever known.

Bartlett, after several efforts to find a place for young Lloyd, finally persuaded Ephraim Allen, the owner and editor of the semiweekly Newburyport *Herald,* to take him on as a printer's apprentice for a term of seven years. Lloyd liked the work, liked Allen, and lived near Bartlett, who filled the place of his father in his life. His mother wrote him long letters of advice (though not often, since postage from Baltimore cost twenty-five cents) and he developed into an adept workman. Allen remembered him as a serious, sober youngster, capable of setting a thousand ems an hour with no more than a few mistakes.

Like Franklin and many other apprentices before him, young Garrison picked up from his trade a great deal of information and a sense of language, partially compensating for his lack of formal schooling. In the evenings he improved his mind with Scott, Byron, Moore, Milton, Pope, and particularly the poetry of Mrs. Felicia Hemans, whose work he imitated in fairly competent youthful stanzas. He joined the Franklin Club, a group of young men devoted to reading, debates, and "self-improvement," and spent a great deal of time in church, avoiding the temptations that beckoned to young apprentices from saloons. Politics interested him, and since Allen exchanged with nearly every other newspaper in Massachusetts, Lloyd read their political articles avidly. Reflecting Allen's own party preferences, he followed the careers of Timothy Pickering and Harrison Gray Otis, Massachusetts's reigning Federalist leaders, with admiration.

Perhaps the only trait that set young Garrison apart from his fellow apprentices was his piety. His mother remarked, when he was with her in Baltimore, that he was already "a complete Baptist in his tenets," and the Baptist

churches of Newburyport knew him as a faithful parish-
ioner. The Reverend Tobias Miller, a Baptist city missionary, worked at his side in Allen's shop, where the two
had long, involved theological discussions. Garrison at sixteen thought seriously of giving his life to missionary
work, and Miller's "beautiful spirit and fine example," he
recalled in later years, had a great influence upon his
mind. Newspaper work won out, however, and in the
spring of 1822 he decided to try his hand at authorship.

One of the more popular items in contemporary newspapers was the essay, a comment on some article of current interest done in the style of Franklin, Addison, or
Steele. An account of a young lady's successful suit for
breach of promise caught young Garrison's eye, and, sign-
ing himself An Old Bachelor, he submitted an essay to
Allen on "Breach of Marriage Promise." Allen unsuspect-
ingly printed it, and during the rest of the year Garrison
continued to hand in other essays from A.O.B. Allen
printed them all, occasionally giving one to Garrison himself to set in type. They ranged over a variety of subjects,
from a philippic against South America to an admiring
bouquet for Harrison Gray Otis.

At last, Allen printed a notice in the paper inviting
A.O.B. to call at the office. After Garrison revealed his authorship, the editor encouraged him to continue his contributions, and since he was an expert typesetter with a
knack for supervision, Allen also made him foreman of
the printing office. For the next two years young Lloyd
wrote what was in effect an irregular column for the *Herald*. His comments were often immature and awkwardly
couched, but after two years of writing he began to develop a vigorous style and a great deal of self-confidence.

Only once, in August of 1822, did he mention slavery in his column, concluding that while its existence did not endanger republican institutions, it seemed unlikely that "much purity, decorum, exactness, and moderation" could "exist in the morals of a people among whom slaves abound."

Letters from Fanny Garrison after 1821 revealed that she was failing in health. In the fall of 1822 she reported the death of her daughter Maria, who had joined her two years before, and she pleaded with her son to visit her. Garrison went to Baltimore in July, 1823, for a three-week visit, finding his mother worn and ill, though indomitably cheerful and optimistic. She was "so altered, so emaciated," he wrote Allen, "that I should not have recognized her, had I not known there were none else in the room." She died on September 3, 1823. Her death affected Lloyd deeply. Years later he wrote, "I always feel like a little boy when I think of Mother," and long after her death he filled his journal with poems to her.

On December 10, 1825, William Lloyd Garrison's apprenticeship expired. At twenty, he was known in Newburyport as a steady, responsible young man, a devout Baptist, a conservative in manners, dress, and politics. Allen agreed to continue his employment while he looked for a position. In the spring of 1826 Garrison found what seemed to be the right opportunity. Isaac Knapp, a young printer in the Gilman printing office in Newburyport, had bought a failing Democratic paper called the *Northern Chronicler;* he renamed it the *Essex Courant* and published it as a neutral political journal, but frequent illness convinced him he needed a partner. Garrison, after discussing the matter with Allen, agreed to join Knapp, with

Allen loaning him the necessary cash. After changing the name to the *Free Press,* an "independent paper," Garrison took over as publisher in March, 1826.

There was nothing to distinguish the *Free Press* from dozens of other struggling New England journals. With Garrison's strong Federalist leanings, he could hardly have been expected to edit an "independent" paper, and the second issue brought a number of cancellations from irate anti-Federalist subscribers. "We beg no man's patronage," Garrison replied editorially, "and shall erase with the same cheerfulness that we insert the name of any individual." Nevertheless the cancellations hurt.

Garrison and Knapp ran the paper with the assistance of one small errand boy, Garrison doing most of the writing, typesetting, and printing. He printed a few essays on nonpolitical topics, including references to "the poor enslaved sons of Africa," but the paper in general was frankly a Federalist organ. Poems by Mrs. Hemans appeared frequently, and a few mediocre poems signed W., written by John Greenleaf Whittier, an East Haverhill shoemaker. But keeping the *Free Press* alive was a losing battle. In the fall of 1826, after six months of struggle, Garrison and Knapp gave up and sold the paper to John Harris, who immediately increased circulation by turning it into a violently pro-Jackson sheet. Garrison stayed on in Newburyport through the year, working as a printer for various firms.

Newburyport offered him no real future either as printer or editor. Boston, the hub of New England and possibly of the universe, as some suspected, offered more. In January, 1827, Garrison left for Boston and finally found work with Lilly and White, an old printing firm.

The city was full of young printers, however, and he found it hard to keep a regular job. Yet Boston life was stimulating to a young man with a religious turn of mind. He attended the Baptist Church on Federal Street, where Howard Malcom preached, but his real favorite was the Reverend Lyman Beecher, who fulminated against Catholics, Unitarians, and theological liberals, to huge congregations at Hanover Street Church. Raised in the hard-shelled Baptism of his mother and Deacon Bartlett, in an atmosphere of soul-searching prayer meetings and thunderous sermons, young Garrison was developing a rigidity of mind and an inflexibility of character that marked him for the rest of his life. The dissenting tradition in which he was reared had no room for halfway measures. Fanny Garrison taught him to read and believe his Bible; Beecher and others in Boston's galaxy of divines showed him how it settled issues.

Garrison found inexpensive lodgings with William Collier, a Baptist city missionary who published a temperance journal, the *National Philanthropist*, under the motto, "Moderate Drinking is the Downhill Road to Intemperance and Drunkenness." Bostonians cared little about temperance in an age of heavy drinking, and Collier knew little about journalism. After a year of indebtedness, he sold his paper to another temperance crusader, Nathaniel White. Garrison, who occasionally helped Collier in setting type, agreed to take over the editorship.

White gave him complete authority over editorial policy, which Garrison used to broaden the paper's scope to include attacks on "religious infidelity," Sabbath mail deliveries, war, tobacco, and immorality. The *Philanthropist*, in the summer of 1828, showed a much more militant

and aggressive spirit than it had had under the gentle
Collier, and its list of subscribers grew. As a full-fledged
editor in the city of Boston (albeit of a very minor journal) Garrison felt he had made a good beginning. He attended every public meeting he could and made himself
known, until the editor of the powerful Boston *Courier*
warned him that obscure young men of his ilk had best
be seen and not heard. Garrison's youthfully self-confident
reply set a pattern for the rest of his journalistic career —
"Let me assure him that if my life be spared, my name
shall one day be known to the world, at least to such an
extent that common inquiry shall be unnecessary."

In March, 1828, however, Garrison met a man who
changed the course of his life. Benjamin Lundy, the antislavery reformer, appeared in Boston and took rooms at
Collier's. Lundy, a New Jersey Quaker, had taken up the
cause of the slave as a young man some twenty years before when, as a harnessmaker in Wheeling, Virginia, he
first saw a slave market. In 1815 he organized an emancipation society in Ohio, and with Charles Osborne founded
a reform paper, the *Philanthropist,* at Mount Pleasant,
Ohio. The *Philanthropist* failed, but Lundy followed it
with the *Genius of Universal Emancipation,* moving the
paper to Tennessee and finally in 1824 to Baltimore,
where it kept up an uncertain and irregular existence.

Antislavery agitation, mild in form and temperate in
aim, had been current in the United States since early
colonial days, guided by such religious leaders as John
Woolman and Samuel Sewall. Not, however, until the formation of the Republic and the enunciation of eighteenth-
century ideals of liberty and equality did the nation give

serious consideration to the slavery question. There were
emancipation bills introduced in Massachusetts in 1776
and 1777, based on the premise that slavery was "contrary
to the laws of nature" and to "natural and inalienable
rights," and the first antislavery petition, presented to
Congress in 1793 and signed by Franklin, declared that
"equal liberty was the portion, and is still the birthright,
of all men." Revolutionary leaders, North and South,
agreed that the slavery was wrong. Jefferson, George Mason, Charles Carroll, William Pinckney, and other Southerners shared antislavery sentiments; more than one slaveholder, like John Pleasants in 1771, freed his slaves from
a conviction that "all mankind has an undoubted right to
freedom," or, like St. George Tucker, planned emancipation schemes based on natural rights doctrines. Eight
states abolished trade in slaves, seven emancipated im-
ported slaves, and the Embargo of 1808, outlawing the
slave trade itself, was the first national victory for antislavery sentiment.

After 1808, manumission, emancipation, and colonization societies flourished in the South, and in the North
Quakers like Elias Hicks and Lundy tried hard to develop antislavery sentiment. Lundy by 1828 had traveled
through nineteen states, leaving antislavery groups behind
him wherever he went. In the border states to the west,
a small group of Quakers, Baptists, and Presbyterians
founded antislavery societies or published struggling papers — John Rankin, James Lockhart, Charles Osborne,
Elihu Embree, in Tennessee; David Rice, James Duncan,
John Crowe, David Barrow, in Kentucky. State societies,
beginning with Pennsylvania's in 1777, appeared in all
states, except the South and Indiana, before 1830. All of

these organizations favored gradual emancipation, since
the immediate abolition of slavery was usually regarded
as impractical and undesirable. Quakers argued that a
boycott of slave-labor products might force the South to
evolve its own method of emancipation. Others recommended that slaves be paid wages, so that they might
eventually purchase their own freedom. Still others recommended the appropriation of state and Federal funds
to buy slaves outright from their masters. From 1794 to
1808 delegates of these societies held national conventions
in Philadelphia, meeting every year except 1799, 1802,
and 1805. From 1808 to 1814 they did not meet, then con-
vened biennially until 1824.

The most popular of all early emancipation schemes
was colonization. The American Colonization Society,
founded in 1817, numbered among its sponsors Henry
Clay, Daniel Webster, James Madison, John Marshall,
and Judge Bushrod Washington, its first president. The
society collected large amounts of money with which to
purchase Negro slaves and resettle them in Africa, sending a few at first to Sierra Leone and later, in 1821, buy-
ing a permanent colonial location in Liberia. The society
hired agents, supported a number of publications (among
them a journal, the *African Repository*) and sent representatives abroad to gather funds to transport 50,000
slaves a year. Colonization proved particularly attractive
to the border states. There, said one Georgian, views were
permitted that were "not a prudent subject of discussion"
in the "Deep South," where the slave population was
larger. Free Negroes and some white antislavery men,
however, protested that colonization was an unsatisfactory

solution to the slavery problem, since it implied that Negroes were both inferior and undesirable. Furthermore, it
simply did not work. After ten years of effort and the ex-
penditure of several millions of dollars, the society had
colonized fewer than 15,000 Negroes, a number replaced
by the birth rate within three months. By the late
eighteen-twenties, some colonizationists had already de-
spaired of success. Furthermore, after 1820 the South became increasingly sensitive to discussions of the slavery
question, which involved not only its morality, but the
economic and political strength of the entire region. The
North already had control of the House of Representatives, and Northern politicians saw a chance to create a
solid bloc of free states that would insure Northern dom-
ination of Congress for generations to come.

The debates over the Missouri Compromise in 1820,
said Jefferson, rang in the South "like a firebell in the
night." As slavery became entangled with westward ex-
pansion and the sectional struggle for political dominance
in the new territories, Southern leaders recognized that
the system formed the very foundation of Southern life.
The rise of cotton, the South's major money crop after
the turn of the century, demanded re-thinking of the
whole problem of slave labor. Cotton was king, and within
a decade the South adjusted its economic and social theories to fit the fact. Cotton meant wealth; cotton needed
slave labor; therefore, the Charleston *Courier* commented, slavery in the Southern states must be protected
as "the great source of their prosperity, wealth, and happiness." Slavery, the South concluded, was necessary, right,
and a "positive good." Southern states vigorously over-

hauled their laws governing slavery, tightened restrictions and plugged loopholes, hoping to make the system secure and impregnable to attack from within or without. On slavery the future of Southern society depended.

A proslavery philosophy had been forming in the South for some time in response to a long-felt need to unify the white population and to separate social and economic classes on color lines. With a solidly proslavery South behind them, the cotton kings and their allies could dominate Southern life by the principle of "divide and rule." Without it, their supply of cheap labor disappeared, class lines dissolved, planter political power weakened. After 1820, the Southern public was subjected to a thorough proslavery propagandizing, while the numerous colonization and emancipation societies gradually disappeared. But most powerful of all as an influence in stifling agitation of the slave question was the compelling argument from private and public safety. The specter of Cato's slave conspiracy of 1739, of Gabriel's plot of 1801, of Denmark Vesey's revolt of 1822 (and later Nat Turner's), hung always over and behind any Southern discussions of slavery. The "Black Terror" of slave revolt (as one legislator remarked in the Virginia House of Delegates) left fear and suspicion "eating into the vitals of every family."

While the South was slowly snuffing out discussion of the slavery question, criticism of the institution increased above the Mason-Dixon line. During the early decades of the century, social and economic changes in the North, particularly the growth of manufacturing, called for ever greater amounts of free labor of a different kind. Nor did slavery suit the farm lands of the new territories to the West, from much of which the system had already been ex-

cluded by the Ordinance of 1787. Hostility to slavery deep-
ened as the great wave of nineteenth-century humanitarian
reform swept the North; British emancipationists, led by
Buxton, Clarkson, Wilberforce, and Zachary Macaulay, attracted American attention and impressed American reformers by their success. Organizational and propagandis-
tic techniques of reform, already worked out by numerous
philanthropic societies in the United States and abroad,
lay ready at hand. All that the abolition of slavery needed
to become a national reform movement was a set of leaders.

Lundy's aim, when he appeared in Boston in 1828, was
"the gradual, though total, abolition of slavery in the
United States." Slaveholders, he believed, if convinced of
the iniquity of the system, would voluntarily free their
slaves if assured of the freedman's resettlement elsewhere.
He had made visits to Canada and Mexico in search of
likely areas for Negro colonies, and he had already managed to start one in Haiti. Traveling constantly through
state after state, Lundy hoped to rally support for emancipation and colonization, especially among clergymen. The
Genius, though nominally published in Baltimore, appeared from any place Lundy happened to be. Walking
from town to town with his pack on his back, he would
stop at a likely print shop, set type, and print and mail
the current issues of his paper. He was not a convincing
speaker, but his obvious sincerity impressed his listeners.
   Lundy's ideas appealed to the young editor. The hard-
ship and loneliness of his own youth made him temperamentally sympathetic to the underdog; Garrison knew
what it was to beg. His talks with Lundy at Collier's simply

reinforced his inner conviction about slavery, and Lundy, in his gentle Quaker way, gave Garrison's tough young mind a principle on which it could act. Before Lundy left Boston William Lloyd Garrison had made his decision. Eleven years later, when Lundy died, Garrison acknowledged the debt. "I feel that I owe everything," he wrote, "instrumentally and under God, to Benjamin Lundy."

Eight Boston clergymen (possibly Channing among them) came to Collier's to hear the Quaker's informal discussion, but "only one or two," Garrison commented, "were for bold and decisive action. . . . Poor Lundy, that meeting was a damper to his feelings." Lundy was a persistent man, and in May of 1828 he returned to Boston for another series of talks. No more successful than before, he left within a few days for a tour of New York and New England, arriving in Boston again in late July. Garrison, fully converted to Lundy's stand, tried to help. He served on a committee to gather signatures for antislavery petitions to Congress, and eventually managed to send one petition to Washington with a hundred names attached.

Getting Boston actively interested in abolishing slavery was not an easy job. The majority of the clergy and their congregations were antislavery in sympathy, while the local chapter of the American Colonization Society was perhaps the largest and strongest in the nation. Colonization seemed an easy and pleasant solution to a delicate problem, but at the same time few New Englanders wished to embarrass or anger Southern slaveholders by undue agitation of the question. By joining Lundy's crusade, Garrison for the first time irrevocably placed himself with the unpopular minority. He never thought of leaving it again.

Copies of Garrison's *National Philanthropist* circulated in temperance circles in Vermont, where the crisp style of its young editor attracted favorable comment. In the summer of 1828, with the Adams-Jackson presidential campaign under way, a delegation of Bennington citizens came to Boston to invite Garrison to take the editorship of a new pro-Adams paper. Garrison did not trust Andrew Jackson, and the *Philanthropist* was in poor financial condition; he gladly accepted the offer and signed a six months' contract on the spot. He added one codicil, however — that he be allowed also to advocate peace, temperance, and emancipation — to which the delegation agreed. The first issue of the Bennington *Journal of the Times* appeared on October 3, 1828, as an "independent" journal, devoted, wrote Garrison, "to the suppression of intemperance and its associate vices, the gradual emancipation of every slave in the Republic, and the perpetuity of national peace."

The *Journal of the Times* opposed Jackson manfully. It was also clear to its readers that much as its editor disliked Jacksonism, he hated slavery more, for nearly every issue had something to say about it. Though he received the news of Old Hickory's election with "melancholy apprehensions" for the future, Garrison went on editing a general reform paper — temperance, observance of the Sabbath, old-fashioned religion, peace, and so on. He gave increasing amounts of space to discussions of pacifism, which appealed to him particularly, and finally announced in his paper, "I heartily, entirely, and practically embrace the doctrine of non-resistance, and am conscientiously opposed to all military exhibitions."

As the months passed, the *Journal* began to look more and more like Lundy's *Genius*. Like Lundy, Garrison favored the gradual emancipation of slaves on grounds of "wisdom and humanity" and as the duty of "every patriot and Christian." Slaveholders, he suggested in the *Journal,* might voluntarily free their slaves if persuaded of the wickedness of the system — particularly if they were reimbursed from Federal funds. The next step, he believed, should be "the transportation of such liberated slaves and free colored people as are desirous of emigrating to a more genial clime" — presumably Haiti or Africa. Before the end of the winter of 1828-1829, the *Journal of the Times* was frankly an antislavery, pacifist paper. "Before God," he wrote, "and our country, we give our pledge that the liberation of the enslaved African shall always be uppermost in our pursuits."

Benjamin Lundy, reading stray issues of the *Journal of the Times,* liked Garrison's style. The *Genius* needed a man of his caliber, and early in 1829 Lundy appeared in Bennington with a proposition. The *Genius,* thought Lundy, would be more effective as a regular weekly; Garrison could be resident editor while Lundy traveled and lectured. Garrison's contract expired in April, and on March 29, 1829, he published his valedictory in the *Journal.* He had been "invited to occupy a broader field, and to engage in a higher enterprise. That field embraces the whole country — that enterprise is in behalf of the slave population." Slavery involved interests of greater moment than any issue which "has come before the American people since the Revolutionary struggle." "I trust in God that I may be the humble instrument of breaking at least one

chain, and restoring one captive to liberty: it will amply
repay a life of severe toil."

Garrison left Bennington for Boston in April, 1829.
Lundy traveled ahead, since he had twelve liberated slaves
to settle in Haiti, and Garrison planned to join him in
Baltimore in late July or early August. In Boston, at Collier's rooming house, he met young William Goodell, who
had come from Providence to merge his religious paper,
the *Investigator*, with White's moribund *National Philanthropist*. Goodell, himself an antislavery man, and Garrison made several calls on local ministers to enlist their
support for the cause of emancipation. They accomplished
little, though the Congregational Society of Boston did invite Garrison to deliver a Fourth of July address in Park
Street Church, a real opportunity for him to present his
case to the most powerful elements in Boston society. He
spent hours writing and revising, and the address, a long
one, established for the first time the bases of his convictions.

After the customary flag-waving introduction, he
launched into an analysis of the state of the nation after
fifty-three years of independence. It was not a pleasant
prospect, he declared — politics was rotten to the core; infidelity, Sabbath-breaking, and intemperance plagued American society. The greatest evil of all was slavery — which
deprived Negroes of their inalienable rights, subjected
them to irresponsible tyranny, and ate at the very foundations of national morality. It was the duty of Christians in
the free states, which were "constitutionally involved in
the guilt of slavery," to "remonstrate against its continu-

ance, and to assist in its overthrow." In this effort, no men possessed the right to use "coercive measures." They must attack the system on moral grounds, for "moral influence, when in vigorous exercise, is irresistible." Slavery, Garrison concluded, could be eliminated only by a great religious crusade, led by the clergy and the churches, and climaxed by the spread into every state of a farflung network of colonization societies. It was an effective speech, well received by a packed audience. Boston knew William Lloyd Garrison when he finished.

Before he left for Baltimore, Garrison made an important decision. He had been, since his first encounter with Lundy, a colonizationist. Nevertheless he had strong doubts, as Lundy himself had, about the colonization scheme. He had also been a believer in gradual emancipation, as Lundy was; immediate emancipation, he said in 1829, was "most assuredly out of the question. . . . No rational man cherishes so wild a vision." But in conversations with Goodell in Boston, Garrison discussed the question of gradual *versus* immediate emancipation thoroughly — and before his departure from Boston he changed his mind.

He arrived in Baltimore with radically different views on the abolition of slavery than those expressed in the Park Street address. He talked with Lundy about his change of heart, and Lundy, unwilling to go quite so far toward immediate emancipation, said: "Thee may put thy initials to thy articles, and I will put my initials to mine, and each will bear his own burden."

The truth of the matter was that the colonization plan was rapidly losing ground among antislavery thinkers everywhere. A few prominent philanthropists, such as Lewis Tappan in New York, regarded the society itself as "a piece of malignant Jesuitry," and Northern Negro leaders like Simeon Jocelyn of Connecticut had fought it since its founding. That, if slavery was a moral sin, it should be immediately and totally abolished was a principle that had occurred to others before Garrison's conversion in 1829. Charles Osborne, John Underhill, and Jesse Willis of the Tennessee Manumission Society declared themselves in favor of immediate Negro emancipation as early as 1815; George Bourne of Virginia, a year later, came out for the "immediate and total abolition" of the slave system. James Duncan's *Treatise on Slavery,* which appeared in Kentucky in 1824, argued for immediatism; John Rankin of Kentucky that same year spoke of the necessity of "emancipation at the present time." For that matter, Lundy himself thought colonization at best an "inadequate" solution; he had even reprinted a British pamphlet, *Immediate, Not Gradual Emancipation,* in his paper in 1825.

American antislavery thinkers, in rejecting colonization for immediatism, were strongly influenced by the example of the British societies, whose program for immediate emancipation of West Indian slaves was on the verge of success. The British Society for the Mitigation and Gradual Abolition of Slavery throughout the British Dominions, which started its aggressive campaigns in 1823, shifted quickly to the principle of immediate emancipation; gradualism, it believed, was simply unworkable, "halfway between now and never." Debates in Parliament had already explored the issue of gradualism versus immediatism thoroughly; the American press gave full coverage to the speeches of the British antislavery immediatists.

British reformers sent thousands of pamphlets to their American friends, corresponded with Americans, and the annual communications from British churches to American congregations of the same denominations often called for quick and decisive action on slavery in the United States. Immediate emancipation of slaves was in the air, and it is not surprising that Garrison should have been infected with it. But what he liked to refer to as "my new and alarming doctrine" was neither new nor exclusively his, though public opinion did regard it as alarming. His doctrine did not, despite his own statement, "burst like a bombshell" on the world.

The first issue of the new *Genius of Universal Emancipation* appeared on September 2, 1829, an eight-page, four-column paper, including a page in French for Haitian subscribers. An American eagle surmounted the title, below it the opening sentence of the preamble to the Declaration of Independence. Garrison's lead editorial informed his readers that the *Genius* would pursue three aims — the overthrow of slavery, the abolition of intemperance, and the outlawing of war. For those of his readers who still favored colonization, he admitted that while he considered the plan "a dilatory and uncertain" method of attacking slavery, he would not oppose it; for his own part he believed all slaves "entitled to immediate and complete emancipation." Since many of Lundy's subscribers were colonizationists, there were a few objections, but Lundy made no attempt to curb his young partner. Garrison, in fact, was not the only immediatist writing for the *Genius*, for Lundy had already appointed Elizabeth Chandler of

Philadelphia to edit a ladies' department, knowing that she too favored immediate emancipation.

What worried Lundy was not Garrison's ideas, but his vehement manner of expressing them. Lundy received a large number of British antislavery publications, and Garrison read them all. The British reformers had developed a savage and bitter style that impressed him, and he began, in his own columns, to reflect it. The initial reactions to Garrison's harshness of language bothered Lundy; after the first few issues, letters of protest began to arrive and the subscription list to diminish. "Where friend Lundy would get one new subscriber," Garrison said later, "I would knock a dozen off." The more he saw of slavery — and there was plenty of it to see on the streets of Baltimore — the more his indignation grew. His abusive attacks on slave traders operating in Baltimore and Washington brought angry letters and threats of reprisal. Austin Woolfolk, a slave trader who some years earlier had given Lundy a brutal beating, drew Garrison's especial ire, and Woolfolk threatened retaliation. Garrison, while admitting to an "impetuous disposition," retorted that "delicacy is not to be counselled. Slavery is a monster, and must be treated as such."

The *Genius* continued, teetering on the edge of bankruptcy. It had subscribers, remarked Lundy wryly, in inverse ratio to good wishes, and Garrison's editorials lost more than they gained of both. Baltimore was a slave-trade center, the harbor filled with ships that carried Negroes like cattle (with mortality rates of 25 per cent) to plantations farther South. That many of these ships were owned by New Englanders and manned by Yankees irked

Garrison. When he saw an announcement that the *Francis,* owned by Francis Todd of Newburyport, Massachusetts, was about to sail for Louisiana with a cargo of slaves, he turned his guns on Todd.

Both Todd and his captain, wrote Garrison in the *Genius,* were "highway robbers and murderers," fit for "the lowest depths of perdition," who should "BE SENTENCED TO SOLITARY CONFINEMENT FOR LIFE." Todd read the article and replied in January, 1830, with a libel suit against Lundy, Garrison, and the *Genius* for damages of five thousand dollars, but a Baltimore Grand Jury had already taken steps. Garrison was indicted, and in February the case of *The State of Maryland* versus *The Genius* began. Argument was heard on March 1, with Charles Mitchell, a Baltimore lawyer interested in antislavery, representing the defendant *gratis.*

The evidence was clear. The jury found for the plaintiff, assessing a fine of fifty dollars and costs, and on March 5 the *Genius* announced the dissolution of its editorial partnership. With all respect to the court's opinion, wrote Garrison, "My pen cannot remain idle, nor my voice be suppressed, nor my heart cease to bleed, while two millions of my fellowbeings wear the shackles of slavery in my own guilty country." Lundy remained sole editor of the *Genius,* which he made once again into a monthly. He continued its publication in Baltimore until his removal to Philadelphia in 1836, and later brought it out in Illinois until his death in 1839.

Garrison, who neither could nor would pay the fine, entered Baltimore City Jail on April 7, 1830, to serve it out. Supervision of prisoners being casual, he wandered about the jail, received visitors, wrote letters to the press, composed sonnets (including one scratched on his cell wall in the best Prisoner of Chillon tradition), and attempted to stir up interest in his case. He prepared copy for a pamphlet, *A Brief Sketch of the Trial of William Lloyd Garrison,* which Lundy published, and corresponded with antislavery friends in Boston, Newburyport, and Baltimore.

The newspapers, however, paid little attention to his imprisonment; he was particularly disappointed that his old employer Allen did not take a stronger stand in his favor in Newburyport, despite Todd's prominence in that city. Arthur Tappan of New York, a wealthy merchant who with his brother Lewis belonged to several reform societies, wrote to Lundy in May, offering not only to pay Garrison's fine but to contribute $100 to the *Genius.* Garrison stepped from his cell on June 5, 1830, after forty-nine days of confinement.

Garrison left Baltimore at once. He went to New York City to thank Tappan, stayed briefly in Newburyport, and then returned to Baltimore to await his second trial on Todd's civil suit. On advice from Lundy he decided not to remain, preferring to allow the case to go by default. A jury later found for Todd, assessing damages of one thousand dollars, but Garrison had long since left. His good-by to Lundy was cool. Lundy blamed Garrison for compromising the *Genius,* while Garrison thought Lundy too gentle and mild to be effective.

In midyear of 1830 Garrison announced that he intended to found a new journal in Washington, the *Public Liberator and Journal of the Times,* devoted to "the abolition of slavery and the moral and intellectual elevation of our colored population." "I shall use great plainness of speech," he wrote, "believing that truth can never be conducive to mischief, and is best discovered by plain words." After mailing copies of his prospectus to lists of antislavery sympathizers in principal cities, he spoke in Philadelphia and New York, in New Haven to Jocelyn's Negro church, and at Amesbury, Massachusetts. In Newburyport, his birthplace, he found Todd there before him. The Presbyterian Church closed its doors to him; the Congregational Church allowed him to use its meeting hall for one lecture, then canceled the second after protests from the church trustees.

The support of the churches, still the dominant element in New England life, Garrison deemed essential. Immediately upon his arrival in Boston, for a lecture, he called on Lyman Beecher, the most powerful of all Boston clergymen, to solicit aid in launching his paper. Beecher refused to help. Garrison's zeal, he remarked, was "commendable," but his direction "misguided." Immediatism would not go in Boston; the majority of clergymen were members of the American Colonization Society and opposed to "fanatical notions." A call on Jeremiah Evarts, Secretary of the Board of Commissioners for Foreign Missions, received the same response, and so did letters to William Ellery Channing, Daniel Webster, and Jeremiah Mason. Garrison's only encouragement came from elderly Abner Kneeland, who gave him the use of his congregation's meeting place, Julien Hall, for his Boston lectures. Kneeland was a freethinker, and his Society of Free Enquirers included more than a few atheists. In return for Kneeland's help Garrison was willing to overlook his "infidelity" and accepted the offer, though it must have strained his Baptist soul to do so.

Garrison's Julien Hall speeches, given on October 15, 16, and 18, were chiefly attacks on the colonization plan and explanations of the urgent necessity for immediate abolition. They drew fairly large audiences, since Garrison's Baltimore jail sentence made him known in Boston reform circles. Beecher himself came, and such men as Samuel Sewall (a young Boston lawyer), John Tappan (brother of Lewis and Arthur), Samuel May (a Unitarian minister from Brooklyn, Connecticut) and Bronson Alcott (May's brother-in-law) attended. Alcott wrote in his journal that Garrison's talks were "full of truth and power," while May found himself completely won over. After the opening lecture he approached Garrison, shook his hand, and said, "I am not sure that I can endorse all you have said this evening. . . . But I am sure you are called to a great work, and I mean to help you." Alcott took May, Garrison, and Sewall home with him, where they talked until long after midnight. Before morning Garrison had three converts. But Alcott's temperament was not suited to organized reform, and he lost sight of abolition among his other enthusiasms. May and Sewall became Garrison's strongest Boston supporters. They hired Athenæum Hall for a fourth lecture, publicized it, and talked abolition to their friends.

The response was so encouraging that Garrison decided to establish his paper in Boston rather than in Washington. "A greater revolution in public sentiment," he said, might "be effected in the free states — and particularly in New England — than at the South." Furthermore, May, Sewall, and Ellis Gray Loring, another young lawyer, promised him financial aid. The three were not inconsequential men in Boston. May, a graduate of Harvard in the famous class of '17, was a descendant of Sewalls and Quincys, and a rising minister in a fashionable parish. Sewall and Loring were prominent lawyers and Unitarians, both successful and wealthy. For Sewall, the cause of the slave had especial appeal; he was a direct descendant of Judge Samuel Sewall, the author of the first antislavery book written in the American colonies. With men such as these behind him, Garrison looked forward with confidence to his task.

Garrison needed help, for he had neither money, type, press, office, nor subscriptions. Isaac Knapp, still rooming at Collier's, had a little money and a job, and, after discussing the matter, decided to enter into a partnership with him. Sewall and Loring advanced capital, while Garrison and Knapp worked out an arrangement with Stephen Foster, a young printer from Maine who was foreman of the *Christian Examiner* print shop. Knapp and Garrison, Foster agreed, could use *Examiner* type in return for help in setting type for the *Examiner;* he also promised to save discarded type for them to use when they could buy their own handpress. The foreman of the *Daily Advocate* shop agreed to let the two use the *Advocate's* press, a supply house promised paper on credit, and May located empty offices at Number 6, Merchants Hall. A few subscriptions came in, including a providential twenty-seven from Philadelphia Negroes sent by James Forten, a free Negro whom Garrison had met during his lecture tour. By the close of 1830, Garrison was nearly ready to go to press.

Garrison could hardly have made a better choice than Boston as the site of his venture. A busy commercial city of more than 60,000, it was astir with new currents of thought. Although Emerson claimed that from 1790 to 1820 Massachusetts produced "not a book, a speech, a conversation, or a thought," he now regarded Boston "as the town which was appointed in the destiny of nations to lead the civilization of North America." The old theological controversies, further complicated by arguments between Unitarian and Calvinist, had produced a new group of liberal-minded clergymen, such as Beecher, Channing, Pierpont, and Henry Ware, all interested in reform. Harvard, emerging from its late eighteenth-century doldrums, was entering a period of greatness; at nearby Cambridge the finest scholars on the continent were producing young men receptive to change, eager to think, pulsing with energy — the Everetts, Bancroft, Ticknor, Emerson, Thoreau, and dozens of others. Boston was alive with ideas, and the tide of the New England Renaissance ran high and strong.

The Boston of 1830 encompassed two worlds. First was the world of Beacon and Brattle Street, stretching to Concord and Cambridge, the world of Emerson and Everett, of Harvard — trained, intellectual, sophisticated divines, and of tightly-knit, aristocratic families grounded in hereditary mercantile wealth — the Lawrences, Abbotts, Lowells, Amorys, and Perkinses. Theirs was a Brahmin world of Congregationalists, Unitarians and transcendentalists, a Federalist-Whig world ruled by the General Congregational Association, Harvard College, Daniel Webster, judges, and merchant princes. The other Boston was a bubbling mixture of artisans and mechanics, tradesmen, immigrants, shopkeepers, laborers. Here Baptists, Methodists, Quakers, free-thinkers, and evangelists met to worship in backstreet churches and rented lofts: a world of exhortatory prayer-meetings, itinerant missionaries, and traveling reformers. Here were Jackson's men, Anti-Masons, Workingmen's Party men, the admirers of Old Hickory and later Little Van — descendants of Sam Adams's rabble and Shays's rebellious farmers.

In this other Boston men worked with their hands and lived on the fringes of poverty. The new industry ruled the destiny of laborer and artisan in ways unknown in earlier America — slums, low pay, long hours, capricious employment. The unskilled laborer could look forward to an average wage of five dollars a week — when he worked — and the skilled artisan might make ends meet with a little to spare. Sensitive to real or fancied injustices, men such as these were ready to listen to reformers. The Garrison children had been born into this world, and grew up in it, on the thin edge of insecurity.

Then too, this other Boston was poor and unlettered, in a society that respected wealth and learning. It was not quite respectable, too yeasty, crude and unstable for Beacon Hill and Cambridge, and one with which it did not readily mix. Emerson, despite his respect for Garrison's cause and for the man himself, remarked to Alcott that he could "never speak handsomely in the presence of persons of Garrison's class." "The spirit and grain of this class is essentially discourteous," Alcott agreed. There was an urgency and desperation in it, a "fight in the blood of the creature." This was Garrison's class, and Garrison's world.

Yet the two Bostons had much in common. Both were constructed out of a deep belief in progress, trust in the individual, faith in the better civilization to come. Emerson's "Trust thyself" and "Nothing is at last sacred but the integrity of your own mind" expressed what both worlds believed. Follow your conscience, set things right, work for progress — this was the Boston creed. Thoreau, Alcott, Channing, Parker, Emerson, Beecher, Garrison — each in his own way reflected it. Garrison, never a man of reflection and thought, followed his conscience to a specific — and to him achingly urgent and eminently practical — reform. The speculations of Emerson and Alcott, or the personal rebellion of Thoreau, were not for him. The cold type of the printer's case was a weapon he could grasp with his hands and turn into flame.

I I

I *Will* Be Heard

NINETEENTH-CENTURY REFORM touched on almost every aspect of American life — education, labor, politics, debt, war, dress, health, family life, church, prisons, the poor, the crippled, and the unfortunate. Horace Mann worked tirelessly for better public education, while Bronson Alcott, George Bancroft, and others experimented with innovations in pedagogy, some European-inspired, some native. Dorothea Dix made her way through the states inspecting prisons and poorhouses, writing precise and damning reports that rocked legislatures. Samuel Gridley Howe of Boston and T. H. Gallaudet of Philadelphia dedicated themselves to improving the lot of the blind and deaf; David Low Dodge of New York and William Ladd of Maine hoped to outlaw war. Fanny Wright, Margaret Fuller, Lucy Stone, the Blackwell sisters, and other strong-minded women campaigned for the rights of women; Amelia Bloomer, agitating for reforms in dress, left her name immortalized in an unlovely article of feminine apparel. Temperance converts, proudly wearing the white badge, paraded by thousands to listen to the impassioned lectures of reformed drunkards like John Hawkins and John B. Gough. Readers of the Scotsman Owen and the Frenchman Fourier planned utopian communities in the rolling farmlands of New England and Ohio, and others, touched by the prevailing religious excitement, founded Christian communist societies based on New Testament injunctions. The American Bible Society, the Society for Foreign Missions, and the American Tract Society sent out agents and lecturers to spread the Gospel around the world. And on the fringes of the reform movement there existed societies to abolish flogging in the Navy, to promote the eating of whole wheat, to abolish corsets, to distribute Bibles to criminals, and to communicate with spirits. There were so many things to do, so little time, and such a long way to go before men lived together in harmony and peace! Nineteenth-century America was in a hurry to have its Kingdom of Heaven in the here and now.

The reform movement had deep roots at home and abroad. Nineteenth-century Americans were direct heirs of the eighteenth-century Enlightenment, with its traditions of natural rights, human equality, and human perfectibility. The Declaration of Independence guaranteed every man a right to life, liberty, and the pursuit of happiness — unjust laws, imperfect institutions, and social disjointures subverted that right. Christianity guaranteed men the right to live as brothers, children of God; a brutally competitive society violated the spirit of Christian ethics. War, drunkenness, poverty, crime, and ignorance nullified those divinely-inspired concepts on which the Republic had been founded. At the same time, Europe provided example and theory for American reformers, for there was in the Western world at large a powerful trend toward recognition of human rights, of the reality of human duties, of the plight of the poor, the oppressed, and the enslaved. Philanthropic groups in England and on the Continent sought out a variety of social and economic ills and strove to cure them by humanitarian efforts. The Reform Bill, the Chartist movement, the Factory Act, the repeal of the Corn Laws, and the West Indies Emancipation Act were successful British attempts at reform, while in Europe and in Latin America the period was dotted with revolutions.

The Romantic Movement reinforced the bequest of "natural rights." The keynote of romanticism was its tremendous and unshakable faith in man, in his capacity to perceive his problems and in his ability to solve them — a faith reflected in the two most representative Americans of the age, Emerson and Jackson. In the individual, the Romantic Era believed, divinity dwelt; to him was revealed truth and right; every man was his own oracle. The American Unitarians and transcendentalists created their deity in man's image — "the idea of God," Channing said, ". . . is the idea of our own spiritual nature, purified and enlarged to infinity."

On another level, the Perfectionists who followed the great evangelist Charles Grandison Finney added their reinforcement to reform. Sin, said Finney, was selfishness; virtue was "disinterested benevolence." Any human being could be saved by the simple process of exchanging selfishness for selflessness. Any human being could attain a state of Christian perfection in this world by his own efforts. But salvation alone, continued Finney, was not enough. The "perfected" one must make his religion active; he must "have the determination to aim at being useful in the highest degree possible." Salvation was not the end but the beginning of a useful life. Finney's theology was, in effect, another affirmation of the belief in progress that permeated the times, and the "doctrine of usefulness" had a direct relationship with contemporary reforms. If Finney's converts searched for ways to make themselves useful, there were a multitude of opportunities ready at hand — particularly in the movement to abolish the sinful, unchristian institution of slavery. They flocked to the abolitionist societies by scores. It was no accident that Finney's two theological seminaries at Oneida and Oberlin eventually produced the majority of abolitionist agents, nor that in its early phases the antislavery crusade had strong overtones of Perfectionist evangelism.

Emerson caught the spirit of his times best. The age moved, he wrote, from the belief "that there is an infinite worthiness in man, which will appear at the call of worth, and that all particular reforms are the removing of impediments." So too Andrew Jackson and his muddy-booted hordes deified the common man as politically sufficient unto himself. "I believe," wrote one politician, echoing Jackson and Emerson (and Finney too), "man becomes more and more endowed with divinity; and as he does he becomes more Godlike in his character and capable of governing himself. Let us go on elevating our people, perfecting our institutions, until democracy shall reach such a point of perfection that we can acclaim with truth that the voice of the people is the voice of God."

Nineteenth-century American reform drew much of its vitality from the militant democracy of the period, from that fervent and complex faith in themselves that de Tocqueville noted in the Americans of 1836. The young nation had survived two wars against the world's greatest military and economic power, created a philosophy of revolution, and built a republic upon it. Democracy was won; the task now remained to consolidate it. Free from entanglements with the decadent societies of the Old World, Emerson's Young Americans eagerly looked forward to creating new ideas and new institutions, or to cleansing old ones of prejudice and evil. In the American concept of democracy, the individual was both a means and a goal. The goal was the complete development of the individual's capacities; the means by which this was to be attained was the reform of every institution or tradition that prevented realization of the individual's powers. In this manner the age of Emerson and Jackson identified nationalism and democracy with progress and perfectibility, providing both a natural and a supernatural basis for reform.

The movement to abolish Negro chattel slavery was part of this pattern, motivated by the same factors that produced the women's rights, evangelical, pacifistic, utopian, humanitarian, and Perfectionist movements. Slavery existed near enough to touch the orbit of every American's life, yet geographically far enough removed from the lives of some to allow it to be judged more or less objectively. It was confined to a portion of the nation whose political and economic interests differed sharply from those of the nonslaveholding sections. The system was politically accessible, subject to state and Federal law. It had obvious religious, social, and moral implications for Americans of every class. At first only one of many reforms, abolition bulked larger and larger in the total, until, at the end, it overshadowed or absorbed nearly all of them.

Abolitionists, and those who sympathized with them, believed slavery to be a direct denial of elementary human rights. When their opponents seemed willing to dispense with the safeguards of the Constitution and to deny the self-evident truths of the Declaration of Independence, the abolitionists gathered more and more support until theirs became the dominant issue of the era. Eventually the issue involved the question of whether the nation would continue to exist, and if so, whether it would remain democratic. It could not, as Lincoln pointed out, endure permanently half-slave and half-free, but would become all one or the other. Before the Civil War came, the abolitionists found themselves allied with a much wider movement to protect the basic rights of democracy — freedom of speech, assembly, and press; academic freedom; the rights of petition and jury trial; freedom of transit and the mails; the entire natural-rights tradition — and to preserve the Union that guaranteed them. "The anti-slavery struggle," Garrison could write quite truthfully in 1852, "was commenced primarily and exclusively with reference to the emancipation of the enslaved inhabitants of the African race in our land; in it now are seen to be included the rights and liberties of all classes of people, without regard to complexion."

The arguments over slavery that developed after 1830 were extremely complex. Antislavery groups were not always able to agree among themselves. Earlier antislavery societies intended to appeal to the national conscience, to change public opinion, and thus to build a great body of Northern and Southern antislavery sentiment that would eventually force the abolition of slavery by legislative action. Their attack on the institution rested on several principles, any one of which might be stressed to the exclusion of others.

First, said some, slavery was immoral and barbaric. The practice of slavebreeding for the market, the refusal of slaveholders to sanction slave marriages or to recognize the slave family as a unit, struck at the very foundations of morality. Relations between master and slave encouraged immoral behavior in Negro and white alike. The system was cruel and inhumane; Theodore Weld's *Slavery As It Is,* Mrs. Stowe's *Uncle Tom's Cabin,* and scores of other studies and novels attempted to document the accusation with stories of whippings, cruel confinements, slave marts, broken families, bloodhounds, and tortures.

Further, slavery was unchristian. Chattel slavery, abolitionists argued, arrogated to one man power over another which rightfully belonged only to God. It was impossible, in the abolitionist view, for a man to be both a slaveholder and a Christian, as it was impossible for an American church to remain Christian while condoning slavery. Such opinions aroused bitter argument within the Protestant churches. The Wesleyan Methodists withdrew from the Methodist Convention of 1843 in protest against its failure to take a stand against slavery, and two years later the Southern Methodists seceded to form the Methodist Episcopal Church, South. The Southern Baptist Convention split on the same issue, while the Presbyterians managed to postpone a division until 1857, when their Southern congregations severed relations.

Next, slavery was undemocratic. It produced a small, powerful class of aristocratic landowners who (abolitionists claimed) had entered into a secret "slave power conspiracy" to extend slavery throughout the nation. The abolitionists carefully charted the progress of this "conspiracy" and issued regular warnings; after the Dred Scott decision of 1857, they pointed out, it needed but one more favorable court decision to achieve its goal. If the Southern "slaveocracy" joined forces with Northern industrial capitalists, abolitionists believed, the two oligarchies together could and would rule the nation — only the abolition of slavery could prevent the combined tyranny of those whom Wendell Phillips strikingly called "The Lords of the Lash and the Lords of the Loom."

Slavery, abolitionists agreed, was economically unsound and wasteful. The poor white man in the South could not compete with unpaid slave labor; so long as slavery existed he would remain poor. And last of all, some antislavery men claimed that slavery was simply illegal, since the Declaration of Independence banned slavery by its affirmation of every man's natural right to life, liberty, and equality. If the Declaration were considered simply a statement of intent, rather than law, abolitionists pointed to the Constitution, which implicitly, at least, banned slavery by outlawing the slave trade. Even if the Constitution did not explicitly abolish slavery, it was because the framers of the document considered it unnecessary to label as illegal an institution already banished by the terms of the Declaration. If the Constitution did actually sanction slavery (as certain commentators believed it might under the guaranteed property clause) the true Christian must perforce obey a "higher law" of morality and reject not only the Constitution but any law based upon it.

Whatever their reasons for believing slavery wrong, all abolitionists believed wholeheartedly that it must be abolished, and soon. They found great difficulty, however, in agreeing on exactly how. One group believed that a national campaign for moral regeneration — an evangelical religious crusade — would cause the abolition of slavery by unanimous consent, North and South. Appeals to the national conscience, thought Theodore Weld, could convince slaveholder and nonslaveholder alike that the system was against God and Christianity. Another school of thought believed that slavery could best be eliminated by working within the existing political framework — either through the two major parties, which could legislate slavery out of existence, or through a third party, which might gain control of the Federal government to accomplish the same end. A third group, believing that the Constitution legalized slavery and that there were no legal means of abolishing it, advocated either abandoning the Constitution for a new one or seceding from any government founded on it. If the Constitution sanctioned an institution which violated "higher laws" of morality and justice, a man must follow his conscience and refuse to remain within the Union founded on that Constitution.

The proslavery forces presented a much more united front than the antislavery organizations. There were always some disaffected areas in the South — western Virginia, western North Carolina, parts of upland Georgia, eastern Tennessee and Kentucky — which refused to follow the lead of the tidewater slaveholders, but proslavery thought in the South was generally fairly well unified after 1830. Antislavery talk was controlled, either by legal intimidation or by social pressure, and the proslavery argument so ceaselessly and efficiently advanced that by 1850 the slaveholding states formed a solid block of opinion.

In order to obtain proslavery solidarity, Southern leaders were forced to infringe on freedom of the press, speech, thought, and education, to encourage and condone mob action, and to appeal to distinctly antidemocratic political, social, and racial theories.

The proslavery argument was both offensive and defensive in nature. In rationalizing the existence of slavery in a free republic, its propagandists were forced to discredit the great Southern liberal tradition and the Declaration of Independence it had produced. Jefferson was presented as an unstable reformer, infected with French radicalism and New England venom; Washington was drawn as a well-intentioned but politically naïve man, taken in by propaganda. The Declaration, said Calhoun, represented an admirable theory but no guide for practical life. Of Jefferson's phrase, "All men are created equal," he remarked, "Taking the proposition literally, there is not a word of truth in it" — a view with which many other Southerners agreed.

Replying to Northern critics, the exponents of slavery cited scriptural, historical, and experiential evidence to prove that men were born actually neither free nor equal. Liberty was not an inheritance granted to every man, they argued, but only to those equipped to deserve it. *Natural* rights to liberty did not exist; men possessed only such rights as society granted them, and what society gave it could take away. As Calhoun explained, men were born into a political and social state, not with natural rights, but subject to the laws and institutions of that state. A Negro, being socially, mentally, and anthropologically inferior to a white man, had no natural rights, deserved none, and could not make responsible use of them. "The Negro," wrote J. B. D. DeBow, "cannot be schooled, nor argued, nor driven into a love of freedom." Southern preachers scrutinized the Bible for arguments justifying slavery as carefully as Northern divines examined Scripture for arguments against it. The Hebrews, it was pointed out, held slaves — white ones.

Having established slavery on religious and political grounds, its supporters went on to prove that its continued existence was necessary and desirable. Slavery was best for the Negro, who needed guardianship and guidance that only some system of servitude could provide. "Providence has placed him in our hands for his good," wrote Governor Hammond of North Carolina, "and has paid us from his labor for our guardianship"; the fact that the Negro failed to appreciate this proved his lack of intelligence. Economically, Southerners maintained, slavery was absolutely necessary to the South and to the nation. The Negro represented a huge investment in property, whose loss would mean financial ruin for one third of the country and probably for the nation itself. And slavery was plainly a social necessity. Only by declassing and subduing the Negro could the white race keep itself safe and racially pure. To grant the black man social status meant miscegenation. Freeing him meant murder, pillage, rape, destruction.

As the years passed, the South produced a flood of proslavery literature proving slavery the best possible system — a "positive good" — that should logically be extended to the North and West, perhaps to white men. "Free society," editorialized the Richmond *Enquirer,* was "in the long run an impracticable form of society." A true democracy (such as the Athenian), wrote Calhoun, could exist only in a clearly stratified society; slavery therefore was "the most safe and stable basis for free institutions in the world." The "demoralized, insurrectionary" free society of the North contrasted ill with the "harmony, union, and stability" of the slave states. There were no starving paupers, no "wage slaves" to foment strikes, no "free love colonies" in states where slavery existed. Senator Downs of Louisiana, echoing Carlyle's sneer at the British abolitionists, challenged anyone "to prove that the white laborers of the North are as happy, as contented, or as comfortable as the slaves of the South." George Fitzhugh of Virginia carried the "positive good" argument to its ultimate conclusion in his *Sociology for the South* (1854) and *Cannibals All!* (1856). One sentence penned by Fitzhugh — "Slavery is the natural and normal condition of the laboring man, whether black or white" — perhaps gave as much help to the abolitionist cause in the North as any that Garrison ever wrote. When war came, Fitzhugh's words seemed to show with unmistakable clarity what the "slave power conspiracy" hoped to create — white slaves in the North and West as well as black ones in the South.

The proslavery argument achieved its purpose well. One antislavery editor in 1855 printed two quotations from the Richmond *Enquirer* side by side. The first, dated 1832, called slavery "a dark and growing evil." The second, dated 1855, called it "a natural and necessary and hitherto universal, hub, element, or institution of society." The difference sprang from twenty years of ceaseless, effective propaganda which, while it served to unify the South, drove a wedge deeper and deeper between the sections.

When Garrison decided to publish his paper in Boston, however, it was still possible to discuss the slavery question without undue heat, as a matter among Northern and Southern gentlemen. The first issue of the *Liberator* appeared on January 1, 1831 — a four-page, four-column folio, fourteen by nine and a quarter inches, printed in boldface, subscriptions two dollars a year. The masthead, in blackletter type, read **Our Country is the World — Our Countrymen are Mankind,** a quotation adapted from Tom Paine. Garrison and Knapp were listed as publishers, Garrison as editor, and Foster as printer.

The front page carried Garrison's first editorial, explaining that his journal favored immediate emancipation of the slave, instead of that "popular but pernicious doctrine of gradual abolition." Acting on "those selfevident truths" contained in the preamble to the Declaration of Independence, the editor asserted his intention to agitate for "the immediate enfranchisement of our slave population," militantly, aggressively, harshly, severely. *"I will be* as harsh as truth, and as uncompromising as justice. On this subject I do not wish to think, or speak, or write with moderation. . . . I am in earnest — I will not equivocate — I will not excuse — I will not retreat a single inch — AND I *WILL* BE HEARD."

The early issues of the *Liberator* caused no great stir in Boston or elsewhere. His paper was received, Garrison said, with "suspicion and apathy," and he found it hard to pay rent. He changed offices in Merchants Hall, moving from Number 6 to 8 to 19 and finally to 11, the cheapest space available. He and Knapp acquired a secondhand press, and, working fourteen hours a day at publishing

time, set up the paper directly from type cases filled
with Foster's discarded type. The editorial offices were
furnished with two chairs, a desk, and a table on which
Garrison often slept. A cake and fruit shop in the base-
ment provided minimum rations, and contributions from
Sewall and Loring paid for the paper and the rent. Arthur
Tappan sent a hundred dollars, and later a letter of credit
for a thousand which Garrison used to pay off debts, only
to go promptly into arrears again. Subscriptions did come
in, however, chiefly from free Negroes in Boston, Philadelphia, and New York.

Since free Negroes had few friends in the North they
responded eagerly to Garrison's prospectus. There were
not many of them, concentrated in the Eastern cities, and
in nearly every Northern state their freedom was severely
limited by "black laws." In Ohio, Indiana, and Illinois
particularly, their civil rights were so circumscribed as to
be virtually nonexistent. In the other Northern states they
faced varying degrees of legalized segregation and discrim-
ination, as well as strong social prejudices. Even liberal
Massachusetts had segregated schools, and some churches
excluded Negroes from white services. The news of a
champion of Negro rights in Boston spread swiftly among
the freedmen. Here was a man who seemed to care. From
the beginning the free Negro formed the core of the *Liberator's* financial support, and until the day of his death its
editor remained a Negro idol, nearly an object of worship.

Garrison listed six subscription agents for his paper in
1831 and fifty-three in 1832, but he admitted that his list
was "more showy than productive." A few visitors climbed
the stairs to Number 11 — some out of sympathy, some out
of curiosity — among them May, Loring, Buffum, Knee-

land, Amos Phelps (pastor of Pine Street Church), Joshua
Coffin, and several fellow editors of minor papers, such
as David Lee Child of the *Massachusetts Journal*, John
G. Whittier of the *New England Weekly Review*, William
Snelling of the Boston *Amateur*, Moses Thacher of the
Telegraph, and Oliver Johnson of the *Christian Soldier*.

Some other Bostonians, as well, took note of Garrison's
violent attacks on the colonizationists. Lyman Beecher,
speaking at a prayer meeting, urged his parishioners to
avoid the "few foolish whites" who stirred up trouble
about slavery. He could not countenance, replied Garrison, any "gradual abolition of wickedness." The question
at hand was one of "right, not expediency, and if the slaves
have a right to their freedom, it ought to be given them,
regardless of consequences." When the Boston Colonization Society rejected his request to speak at their meetings,
Garrison retaliated by redoubling his attacks on them.
The whole colonization scheme, he wrote, was "wrong in
principle and impotent in design." "Search the records of
heathenism," he said, "and sentiments more hostile to the
spirit of the Gospel and of a more black and blasphemous
complexion than these, cannot be found."

The tone of the *Liberator's* editorials worried May, who
suggested diplomatically that Garrison might do well to
temper his language. "My language," he replied, "is exactly such as suits me; it will displease many, I know — to
displease them is my intention." In the seventeenth number Garrison added a new ornamental masthead, a crude
cut of a slave auction in Washington, with the capitol in
the distance, the American flag inscribed with "Liberty"
floating above it, and a slave at a whipping post beside it.
Neither Sewall nor May approved, but the same cut re-

mained, with variations, for the rest of the *Liberator's* life. "There shall be no neutrals," Garrison said. "Men shall either like me or dislike me."

A few malicious or threatening letters arrived. One from Princeton, New Jersey, opened with "You damned scoundrel," and another, from the South, promised that "Your paper cannot be much longer tolerated." These Garrison proudly reprinted. "Nothing but my own death, or want of patronage," he noted, "shall stop the *Liberator*." Other letters came from antislavery men who took exception to his language; these he treated with courtesy, writing long explanations justifying his course. President Wayland of Brown University, an eminent divine, told him, "The tendency of your paper is to produce rebellion. Its attitude to slave-owners is menacing and vindictive. The tendency of your remarks is to prejudice their minds against a cool discussion of the subject." It made no difference to Garrison. "Religious professors of all denominations must bear unqualified testimony against slavery," he replied, lest "they share in the guilt of its existence."

Arthur Tappan, whose letters encouraged Garrison during the early months of 1831, approached him in June with an attractive offer. Simeon Jocelyn of New Haven hoped to found a manual training school for free Negroes; Tappan had already pledged ten thousand dollars, bought land, and secured promises from Yale faculty members to teach in the school. Would Garrison and the *Liberator* assist in the venture, and would he attend, with Tappan and Jocelyn, the first Annual Convention of Colored People in Philadelphia? Garrison was pleased to accept, for Tappan's friendship was extremely important, and new subscribers to the *Liberator* were much to be desired. In late June he went to Philadelphia at Tappan's expense, spoke to the convention, and made substantial additions to his subscription list. The convention pledged another ten thousand dollars to Jocelyn's school, but the city of New Haven was less enthusiastic. A town meeting, declaring that "the founding of colleges for the education of colored people is an unwarranted and dangerous interference with the internal concerns of the South," voted that Jocelyn's school "ought to be discouraged." The plan was dropped, but neither Garrison nor Tappan was willing to give it up completely.

In early August of 1831 Garrison told a friend, "I was never so happy and confident in my mind as at the present time," despite the fact that the debt-ridden *Liberator,* read only by a few Bostonians and a few hundred free Negroes, existed chiefly by the largesse of Sewall, Loring, Tappan, and others of the faithful. On August 13 a Negro preacher named Nat Turner, in Southampton, Virginia, led a slave revolt that left fifty-seven white people dead and set a blaze of fear running through the South. The whole plot, Governor Floyd of Virginia announced, was "undoubtedly designed and matured by unrestrained fanatics in some of the neighboring states." Since the most unrestrained fanatic at hand was William Lloyd Garrison, the connection was simple. Turner was led on, wrote the Tarborough, North Carolina, *Free Press,* by "an incendiary paper, the *Liberator,* published in either Boston or Philadelphia by a white man, with the avowed purpose of exciting rebellion in the South." One by one Southern newspapers picked up the charge until the South was filled with clamor against Garrison. There was little doubt, wrote one Southerner, that Garrison had not much longer to live — "think not you can avoid the blow, for poison will accomplish what the dagger may fail of effecting."

Garrison, by his own admission, had "not a single subscriber South of the Potomac," and no Southern agents. He did exchange with some one hundred Southern editors, following contemporary journalistic practice. To the Southern editors who read it, the *Liberator* illustrated the very worst aspects of Northern abolitionist opinion, while Garrison's prose lent itself admirably to juicy quotation. Consequently the South received, from its own press, the impression that Garrison represented a far larger influence in Northern antislavery circles than he did, and thousands of Southerners who had never heard of Garrison before Nat Turner's revolt laid the responsibility for it at his office door. The obscure reformer, toiling in a barren Boston loft, suddenly emerged as the arch-symbol of antislavery extremism, the leader of Northern abolitionist sentiment, a "murdering hound," an "infamous wretch," and an "incendiary plotter."

The fact was that Garrison was a nonresistant pacifist, opposed to violence in any form. While working for Lundy in 1829, he had publicly censured David Walker's incendiary pamphlet, *An Appeal to the Colored Citizens of the World*. In the first number of his *Liberator* he had warned the slaves poetically:

> Not by the sword shall your deliverance be;
> Not by the shedding of your masters' blood.

He denied any knowledge of or responsibility for Turner's ill-advised plot. "It is not the real or avowed object of the *Liberator* to stir up insurrectionism, but the contrary," he explained. "Nothing can be more fatal to our hopes . . . than such silly, phrenzied, anti-Christian proceedings." Yet Turner's act, Garrison believed, contained a lesson for the South. The slave, so long as slavery existed, would continue to threaten the slaveholder with "dreadful retaliation." "If we would not see our land deluged in blood, we must instantly burst the shackles of slaves. . . . IMMEDIATE EMANCIPATION can alone save [the South] from the vengeance of Heaven and cancel the debt of ages."

Garrison's disclaimers convinced no one. The Vigilance Committee of Columbia, South Carolina, offered a reward of fifteen hundred dollars for the apprehension and conviction of anyone found circulating the *Liberator*. Georgetown, in the District of Columbia, passed a law fining any free Negro who received the *Liberator* in the mails. In Raleigh, North Carolina, Garrison and Knapp were indicted *in absentia* for inciting slaves to revolt. The Georgia legislature voted five thousand dollars to anyone who would produce Garrison in Georgia for arrest and prosecution; the *National Intelligencer* in Washington proposed that he be extradited to Virginia for trial. Governor Hamilton of South Carolina sent a special message to the legislature, accompanied by sample copies of the *Liberator*, proving that "the spirit of insubordination" exhibited by Turner "was excited by incendiary newspapers and other publications, put forth in the non-slaveholding states." Laws appeared on Southern statute books, forbidding anti-slavery opinion, banning Negro schools, outlawing anti-slavery societies, tightening controls over slaves. The Virginia legislature, engaged in a series of crucial debates over slavery in the winter of 1831-1832, defeated proposals for emancipation by a small majority. As one Virginian wrote bitterly, men such as Garrison placed new difficulties in the way of "all judicious schemes of emancipation, by prejudicing the minds of slaveholders."

The sounds of uproar in the South echoed in Boston. Senator Robert Hayne of South Carolina, after reading a copy of Garrison's paper, wrote directly to Mayor Harrison Gray Otis to demand action against the editor. Otis was forced to admit with some embarrassment that he knew neither Garrison nor his publication. He sent an investigator to the *Liberator* offices, who reported that the tempest over the paper was highly unjustified. It was supported, Otis told Hayne, "by a very few insignificant persons of all colors . . . edited by an individual who formerly lived at Baltimore, where his feelings have been exasperated by some occurrences consequent to his publications there." Garrison's zeal "had not made, nor was likely to make proselytes among the respectable classes of our people."

There was a great deal of truth in Otis's reply. The *Liberator* had only fifty white subscribers, probably no more than half of them in Boston, and those Garrison's personal friends. What Boston needed, Garrison told May and Sewall, was a local antislavery organization, not only to furnish financing for the *Liberator* but to gain adherents to the cause. Sewall agreed to call a meeting for November 13, 1831, to discuss the formation of an abolitionist society, and that evening fifteen men met at Sewall's law offices to hear Garrison's proposal. The British societies, he reminded them, succeeded only after they adopted the principle of immediate emancipation; America needed a network of similar societies, founded on the same doctrine.

Samuel May, who was there, reported later that nine of the fifteen favored immediatism; Oliver Johnson's impression was that while the six doubters really favored it, they believed it wiser to proceed with caution. The meeting took no action and recessed until December 16, when ten men met again in Sewall's office. Five of the original group came, plus three converts and one man who still remains unidentified — David Lee Child, Loring, Isaac Child, Robert Hall, John Cutts Smith, Oliver Johnson, Knapp, Joshua Coffin, Sewall, and Garrison, with May absent. Of these Hall and Smith (local ministers), Coffin (a teacher), and Isaac Child (David's brother) were recent additions to the cause. The group agreed to accept immediate emancipation as the new organization's guiding principle, and appointed David Child, Sewall, Loring, Johnson, and Garrison as a committee to draft a constitution. Garrison reported the committee's progress in the *Liberator,* announcing that the final organization meeting would be held on January 1, 1832.

The January meeting ran into difficulties. Five more men appeared, including Alonzo Lewis (a poet and teacher), William Snelling of the *Amateur,* Abijah Blanchard (an anti-Masonic editor), and Amos Phelps and Gamaliel Bradford, both ministers. The meeting adopted the body of the constitution but several men objected to the aggressive language of the preamble. Sewall, Garrison, Blanchard, and Snelling were directed to rewrite it for reconsideration at another meeting on January 6. At this meeting Smith, Isaac Child, May, and Blanchard did not appear, but Arnold Buffum, John Fuller, Moses Thacher, Stillman Newcomb, Benjamin Bacon, George Odidone, Henry Stockton, and M. H. Simpson came — all ministers, law-

yers, merchants, and teachers, and men of some standing
in the city.

According to the revised preamble, the new society favored "immediate freedom from personal bondage of
whatsoever kind, unless imposed by the sentence of law,
for the commission of some crime." Its members pledged
themselves to proceed "by peaceful and lawful means" and
to give "no countenance to the violence of insurrection."
An hour of discussion sufficed to iron out minor disagreements. In the final vote Sewall, Loring, and Child decided
to vote against the preamble, claiming its language might
alienate Boston opinion, but they did promise their cooperation. With the constitution adopted, the meeting then
chose its officers, mostly by acclamation. Buffum, a Quaker
hat manufacturer converted to immediatism by the British,
became president, Garrison secretary, Coffin recorder, and
Simpson treasurer. Thacher, Fuller, Johnson, Hall, Bacon,
and Sewall composed the executive council. "Our numbers are few," remarked Garrison, "and our influence limited, but . . . we shall shake the nation by their mighty
power." The New England Antislavery Society was a
reality.

The *Liberator* published the preamble and constitution
of the society, announced regular monthly meetings, and
set an annual business meeting for the second Wednesday
of each January. The council designated the *Liberator* as
the official organ of the society, authorized the appointment of agents for lectures, and planned the distribution
of pamphlets. For a rent of fifty-six dollars a year Garrison
found a large room at 46 Washington Street and parti-
tioned it into a lecture room and a small office. Bacon, May,
and Phelps offered to help with correspondence. Thacher,

a Presbyterian minister, circulated an appeal for funds and obliged Garrison by writing a long attack on the colonizationists for the *Liberator*. Buffum took a commission as lecturer (to collect his own salary) while Garrison accepted a similar post for a period of three months at two hundred dollars, the first salary he had ever received for his abolitionist efforts. In the spring of 1832 he toured central and eastern Massachusetts, northern Rhode Island, and southern Maine, publicizing the society and adding to the *Liberator's* subscription list.

The first major task of the New England Antislavery Society was to put the final quietus on the Boston colonizationists. Garrison, therefore, published a thick pamphlet, *Thoughts on African Colonization: or an impartial exhibition of the doctrines, principles, and purposes of the American Colonization Society, together with the resolutions, addresses, and remonstrances of the free people of color.* "I shall have occasion," he wrote in the preface, "to use very plain and sometimes very severe language." (Of this his readers had no doubt.) The Colonization Society, he charged, was a proslavery organization "solemnly pledged not to interfere with a system unfathomably deep in pollution," nourished on "fear and selfishness," encrusted with "corroding evil."

His attack was harsh, and his language aroused apprehension among the New England Society's scanty membership. There was no reason to malign one's neighbors, May thought, and Garrison's epithets stirred a good many conservative Bostonians. Tappan in New York, however, read the pamphlet with satisfaction and asked for a hundred copies. Invitations to lecture came in, particularly from

Negro groups, and the *Liberator's* fortunes improved. His strictures against colonization, combined with the attacks emanating from the South, made Garrison unquestionably the outstanding figure in New England antislavery circles. The distribution of his paper was small, and the New England Antislavery Society was a miniscule drop in a sea of reform, but by the end of 1832 no one in New England who believed in immediate emancipation of the slave could challenge William Lloyd Garrison's position as a leader.

But what Garrison was doing in New England, a larger, better-organized, and better-financed group was doing with greater skill in New York City. New York was, and had been for thirty years, the center of numerous charitable and reform societies. Thousands of delegates met in the city at the annual reform society conventions, and there too were the headquarters of "The Great Eight" major benevolent organizations. Few men were better known in reform circles than Arthur and Lewis Tappan, who had come from Massachusetts to New York to develop a profitable trade in silks, found the *Journal of Commerce,* open a store, and amass a fortune. The Tappan brothers "loved unpopular causes" and contributed heavily to a variety of reforms. Deeply religious, both men were ardent converts to the evangelistic doctrines of Charles Grandison Finney; they founded "free churches" for his congregations, contributed large sums to his seminaries, and built the Broadway Tabernacle especially for his "holy band." In 1830 Arthur organized the Association of Gentlemen, a group of wealthy New Yorkers, to underwrite the *Evangelist,* a weekly paper devoted to reform in general and Finney's theology in particular. Joshua Leavitt, an ordained minister, a Yale graduate, and an agent for the Seaman's Friend Society, came to New York as its editor. "The accumulation of property for selfish purposes," the *Evangelist* stated in one of its early issues, "is repugnant to the Gospel." Therefore the Association of Gentlemen entered "into a solemn agreement not to lay up any property we may hereafter acquire . . . but consecrate the whole of it to the Lord." The Lord's work was reform.

The Tappans, searching for a way to consecrate their wealth, soon discovered slavery. As near-professional reformers, they were both thoroughly familiar with the work of the British emancipationists long before Garrison read Lundy's files in Baltimore, and neither approved of the American Colonization Society. In early 1831, believing that it was time to do something about slavery in the United States, Arthur Tappan called a meeting in New York of Theodore Weld, Joshua Leavitt, Simeon Jocelyn, William Goodell, and the Reverend George Bourne. Goodell, a professional reform journalist, had moved his Boston *Philanthropist* to New York a year before. Weld, a disciple of Finney's, was currently at Oneida Institute in upper New York, training himself to preach Finney's Perfectionist theology. Bourne, known as "Father Bourne" to antislavery men, had been an active abolitionist since 1816. All of them had heard of Garrison. None, however, with the exception of Arthur Tappan and Goodell, knew him well; nearly a year and a half later Weld was to write that he was "ignorant of the history, the specific plans, modes of operation, present position, and ultimate aims" of Garrison's Boston group. The topic of their discussion was the advisability of founding a national anti-slavery society — not a new idea, since it had been the subject of talk at the annual reform meetings as early as 1828.

Encouraged by the informal meetings in spring of 1831, Tappan proposed to the Association of Gentlemen in June, nearly a year and a half before the New England Anti-slavery Society adopted its constitution, that a national antislavery society, modeled on the British plan and dedicated to the immediate abolition of slavery, be founded in New York. The Gentlemen favored the suggestion, and as a first step agreed to sponsor Jocelyn's New Haven school. Jocelyn's school failed to materialize; Turner's revolt made antislavery societies unpopular in New York as well as in the South; the debates in the Virginia legislature showed the temperature of Southern opinion all too clearly. The New Yorkers, therefore, decided to suspend the organization of the proposed society until the signs were more auspicious. The American Colonization Society, well aware of the Tappans' plan, sent its agent, Elliot Cresson, to England to counteract any influence the proposed new society might exert on the British. Cresson, however, met the opposition of Charles Stuart, a Jamaica-born Englishman who had once labored in Finney's cause in the United States. A close friend of Weld's, Stuart fought Cresson every step of his way, and by 1831 he had set the London Antislavery Society and its leaders against the American colonizationists.

Arthur Tappan usually had more than one iron heating in the reform fire. Still searching for ways to help Finney, he planned to establish in the West a manual training

school that would also serve as a seminary for training
Finney's young preachers. He hired Weld as agent for the
school, and in the fall of 1831 Weld toured the South and
West, gathering support for Tappan's plan and making
abolitionist converts along the way. In Alabama he met
and convinced James G. Birney, a prosperous slaveholding lawyer, who disposed of his slaves and accepted an
agency for the American Colonization Society, the only
organization of its kind still functioning in the South. Discouraged with colonization, Birney soon resigned and
moved to Kentucky, where he tried to organize an emancipationist society of his own. At Western Reserve University in Ohio, Weld met another antislavery group, led by
Elizur Wright, junior, Beriah Green, and President
Charles Storrs, all faculty members. In spring of 1832
Weld finally found, at Cincinnati, the site he was looking
for—Lane Seminary, a theological school badly in need of
funds. Tappan approved the choice and began to hire a faculty. For president he chose Lyman Beecher, though
Beecher's liking for the colonizationist cause gave Arthur
serious misgivings. Young men from Finney's entourage
began to arrive in Cincinnati, many of them already ardent antislavery sympathizers — such as Marius Robinson
of Tennessee, Henry B. Stanton of upstate New York,
James Thome of Kentucky, and of course Weld himself.

While the New York and Ohio antislavery groups were
mobilizing, Garrison pursued an independent course in
New England. In January, 1833, he received a letter from
Prudence Crandall, a young lady in Canterbury, Connecticut, which explained that she was an enthusiastic

reader of the *Liberator* and that she soon hoped to open a
school for Negro girls. Garrison printed an announcement
that Miss Crandall would open a "high School for young
Colored Ladies and Misses," commenting that she deserved the support of "every right-thinking citizen." A
town meeting in Canterbury decided otherwise, resolving
that "the nation with all its institutions of right belong to
the white men, who now possess them," and warning
Miss Crandall that a Negro school would not be tolerated.
Miss Crandall nevertheless opened her school, with about
twenty girls in attendance; shops refused to sell her food,
her windows were broken, and the school's well was filled
with manure. Local officials attempted to prosecute her
students under an old vagrancy law, but dropped the case
when Samuel May of nearby Brooklyn came to her rescue.

In May, 1833, Andrew Judson, a Canterbury lawyer and
an official of the local Colonization Society, persuaded the
Connecticut state legislature to pass a law forbidding the
instruction of Negroes in private schools, a law aimed directly at Prudence Crandall. At the urging of Garrison and
May, she consented to make herself a test case, continued
her school, and in August was arrested and jailed. The
case was made to order for the *Liberator*. Garrison
spread running accounts of it over his paper for months,
in language so abusive that Miss Crandall herself asked
him to soften his attacks. Canterbury citizens threatened
him with libel suits for his remarks about the town's
"moral nondescripts," and eventually five such suits were
brought, involving him in legal tangles for the next two
years. When the Crandall case came to trial in late 1833,
the best that her three lawyers, sent by Arthur Tappan,

could do was to procure a hung jury. At a second trial, held in mid-1834, Miss Crandall was convicted. Eventually the decision was appealed and quashed, but she found the town so hostile that she gave up teaching, married, and moved to Illinois. But by that time Garrison was deep in another kind of battle.

I I I

Ours Is a Moral Crusade

EARLY IN 1833 Garrison received an announcement of a World Antislavery Convention in London. The trip was to be a turning point in his career, and was to project him into a place of central importance in the antislavery movement — but when the invitation came he had neither authority nor money to make the journey. Authority was not hard to obtain: his own New England society obligingly named him its official delegate. The New York group of the national society, however, refused to approve or to finance his mission, since it had already chosen its own delegates. Garrison quickly refurbished Jocelyn's plan for a Negro school and proposed that he be sent to England to raise money for it. He addressed the Annual Convention of the Free People of Color and advertised in the *Liberator*, explaining that he would collect funds for Jocelyn, discredit Cresson (who was "duping the British out of large sums of money"), and establish "a union of sentiment and action" with British emancipationist leaders. He gathered about six hundred dollars, enough for a one-way ticket and expenses.

Garrison sailed from New York on May 2, 1833, sending reports to the *Liberator* of the dangers that sur-

rounded him in that city. He was "watched and hunted,"
he claimed, by proslavery men and colonizationists; he ex-
posed a plot to assassinate him, and hid with friends.
While waiting for passage, he said, he talked to Tappan
and the New Yorkers and "convinced them of the necessity
of founding a national antislavery society," although the
New Yorkers had convinced themselves nearly two years
earlier. The stories made good copy and his readers were
impressed.

Garrison arrived in England at exactly the right time.
The West Indies emancipation bill seemed about to pass
and British abolitionists were in an exalted mood. Garrison's name was familiar through his pamphlet on colonization and through Turner's revolt, and when he presented
his credentials the London Antislavery Society unquestion-
ingly accepted him as the leader of American abolitionism. He sent a challenge to Cresson to engage him in public debate (which Cresson refused) and followed it with
an abusive letter to *The Times* on the colonizationists.
Meanwhile he consulted with the British emancipationists
and spoke frequently and well at public meetings, ladling
invective onto Cresson and the American Colonization Society. James Cropper and George Thompson arranged
meetings for him and accompanied him on his tour. He
and Thompson took to each other at first sight. Thompson, who had studied for both the bar and the ministry,
was an immediate abolitionist and one of the London society's most brilliant speakers, as uncompromisingly aggressive as Garrison himself.

Garrison called on Wilberforce, Macaulay, Buxton, and
Daniel O'Connell, and got their signatures on an anti-
colonization petition. He spoke on American slavery at

Exeter Hall to a huge crowd, wringing British hearts with accounts of "the perils I have risked, the persecutions encountered, the sufferings endured," and he reported (not quite accurately) that abolition societies were springing up "in every part of the United States . . . on the principle of immediate and unconditional emancipation." He drew most applause for his ringing indictment of America. "I accuse the land of my nativity," he said, "of insulting the majesty of Heaven with the grossest mockery that was ever exhibited to man . . . of giving open, deliberate, and base denial to her boasted Declaration of Independence . . . suffering a large portion of her population to be lacerated, starved, plundered . . . trafficking in the bodies and souls of men, of legalizing on an enormous scale licentiousness, fraud, cruelty, and murder." By the time he was ready to leave in late September he had convinced the British that he was the spearhead of a swiftly growing American abolitionist movement. Since the Boston and New York papers followed his course in England with great interest and mounting indignation, he had also very nearly convinced a large segment of American public opinion as well.

Elliot Cresson's dispatches to the New York newspapers kept the American public well informed of these activities. Garrison's "abolitionist ravings," said the *Evening Post,* were as "mad as the winds," but his remarks about his native land were worse. His sole purpose abroad, wrote the *Commercial Advertiser,* seemed to have been to "traduce the people and institutions of his own country." Another writer prophetically described him as a man obviously "willing to trample the Constitution under foot." A handbill in Boston, welcoming him home from his "disgraceful mission," accused him of "slandering Americans to the utmost of his power"; he stood arm in arm, said another paper, with that notorious archenemy of Americans, Daniel O'Connell, and had "recommended to slaves that they cut their master's throats." Members of the American Colonization Society fumed over his accusation that their organization was "steeped in sin, [and] deep in pollution."

Garrison embarked for home in September, borrowing his fare from a Negro friend of Tappan. During his absence, the Tappans, Leavitt, Goodell, and Rankin, with Green and Wright from Ohio, had decided to establish a New York City antislavery society as the first step toward a national organization. They had announced a meeting at Clinton Hall on October 2. Before that date, the city was placarded by signs, signed "Many Southerners," urging all citizens opposed to immediate abolition to attend to break up the gathering. Sensing trouble, Tappan then changed the meeting place to Chatham Street Chapel. On the appointed evening, a large crowd assembled at Clinton Hall — found it empty, and held an anti-abolitionist session of its own. When it was over, most of the crowd moved to Chatham Street Chapel, but the abolitionists had already finished. Garrison, who landed that evening, joined the mob outside Clinton Hall but did not identify himself, and left for Boston the next morning without calling on the New Yorkers. Nevertheless, he assumed that his arrival had called out the mob. "As soon as I landed," he wrote, "I turned the city of New York upside down. Five thousand people turned out to see me tarred and feathered, but were disappointed."

The New Yorkers were not the only ones interested in founding a national antislavery society. During the summer of 1833 the Philadelphia abolitionists discussed the matter and, after a preliminary meeting, sent Evan Lewis to New York to propose that the Tappans make the first move. The success of the British emancipation bill made it imperative that the Americans take advantage of favorable public opinion; in September of 1833, therefore, shortly before the formation of the City Society, the New York group announced an organizational convention for early 1834. Garrison protested strongly — there was no time to lose — and the Tappans obligingly changed the date to December, 1833. In deference to the Philadelphians, Arthur Tappan suggested that their city be the site of the meeting, mailing out invitations to all "friends of immediate emancipation" to meet in Philadelphia on December 4 "to form a NATIONAL ANTISLAVERY SOCIETY."

Garrison organized his Boston delegation — Coffin, Philips, May, Southard, Buffum, and others — and joined to it small contingents from Maine and Connecticut. Between fifty and sixty delegates appeared at Adelphi Hall in Philadelphia on the appointed date. There were perhaps a dozen Congregational or Presbyterian ministers, May reported, a few Unitarians, a few Negroes, and several Quaker women from Philadelphia, including the well-known Lucretia Mott. Beriah Green of Ohio was elected president of the convention, Lewis Tappan, William Green and Whittier secretaries, and the speeches began.

Lewis Tappan had earlier expressed the hope that Garrison's name might not be "inserted prominently" in the proceedings, lest it "keep away many professed friends of abolition." It was difficult, however, to keep Garrison, with the blessing of the victorious British emancipationists still bright on him, from taking the lion's share of the praise. Lewis himself finally offered a resolution, which was met with resounding applause, to honor Garrison as "one who has the confidence of the people of England."

The New Yorkers nevertheless did not intend to allow Garrison to dominate the meeting if they could prevent it. The first business of the convention was to appoint committees to nominate officers and to draft a constitution. Garrison was on neither. The nominating committee offered Arthur Tappan as president of the new society, Lewis Tappan as a member of the Executive Committee, Elizur Wright as secretary, William Green as treasurer — all from the New York group — with Garrison in the minor post of Secretary of Foreign Correspondence.

The committee to draft a constitution presented its report on the fourth. The first article set the tone, affirming that "slaveholding is a heinous crime in the sight of God, and that the duty, safety, the best interest of all concerned, require its immediate abandonment, without expatriation." The society further pledged itself to "the entire abolition of slavery in the United States" and while it admitted that the states alone possessed legislative power over the institution, expressed the hope that "arguments addressed to the understandings and consciences" of the slaveholders themselves, might convince them of "the moral sin of slavery," and led them to take steps to eradicate it at once. Congress, meanwhile, was advised to abolish the system in the District of Columbia and to outlaw the interstate slave trade. Finally, the constitution pledged the society to "discountenance the use of force" in pursuing its work.

While the draft was perfectly satisfactory to the convention, some members, feeling the need of "a document of more imposing character," suggested that another committee draw up a Declaration of Sentiments (customary in reform societies) to publish the society's aims in more effective terms. May, Garrison, and Whittier were named a subcommittee to draw up such a statement, and the three men repaired to the home of James McCrummell, a local free Negro, to discuss it. At ten o'clock that night Garrison began the task of composition, and handed his draft, with a few alterations, to the full committee the next morning.

The committee discussed Garrison's work for three hours. Some objected to its "severity of language," others to its attack on the American Colonization Society. The majority was dubious of its effect on public opinion, believing it a far too comprehensive indictment of North and South to inspire wide support. It was difficult, though, to argue against it, for Garrison posed the issues in terms that no one on the committee could conscientiously deny. His language was harsh, but still it had the ring of sincerity and truth. Garrison defended it eloquently, and his draft suffered only minor changes; with the most scathing references to the colonization deleted, it reached the convention floor in the early afternoon. The convention spent the entire afternoon discussing it. Garrison's prose aroused objections, as it had in committee, but again few could say "no" to the propositions it advanced. Both the New Yorkers and the Pennsylvania Quakers favored softer language, but finally the meeting ordered Dr. Abraham Cox, an expert penman, to inscribe it on parchment. The next morning every member signed it except the women.

The Declaration of Sentiments was Garrisonian rhetoric at its best. "Ours," he wrote, "is a moral crusade," to lift in the land "the voice of remonstrance, of warning, of entreaty, of rebuke." "Ours shall be such only as the opposition of moral purity to moral corruption—the destruction of error by the potency of truth—the overthrow of prejudice by the power of love—and the abolition of slavery by the spirit of repentance." Therefore, Garrison continued, the society believed that "the slaves ought instantly to be set free, and brought under the protection of the laws"; and all who owned and kept slaves should be known to the world as "man-stealers"; that the "highest obligation" rested on the free states "to remove slavery by moral law and political action, as prescribed in the Constitution"; and that "those laws now in force, admitting the right of slavery, are therefore, under God, utterly null and void, being an audacious usurpation of the Divine Prerogative, a daring infringement on the law of nature, a base overthrow of the very foundations of the social compact . . . and a presumptious transgression of all the holy commandments."

The new American Antislavery Society made its headquarters in New York, in offices at the corner of Nassau and Spruce Streets. Arthur Tappan threw his fortune into its treasury, contributing a thousand dollars a month for many months. The society took over the *Emancipator,* an ailing reform weekly, hired William Goodell as editor, and appointed agents to canvass the nation for funds.

Garrison, back in Boston, took much of the applause. "By dint of some industry and much persuasion," he told the New England society, "I succeeded in inducing the

abolitionists in New York to join our little band in Boston
in calling a national convention" — a neat reversal of
roles.

Garrison's willingness to accept full credit for the Philadelphia convention created the suspicion in New York
that he might prove to be the national society's cowbird,
pushing the Tappan eggs out of the nest. The executive
committee ordered all letters written by him as Secretary
for Foreign Correspondence to be first submitted to the
committee for approval. Garrison, chafing at this restraint,
resigned the position within a month. Furthermore, Tappan made tentative suggestions that the *Liberator* be
merged with the *Emancipator,* a move Garrison quickly
blocked. The *Liberator,* he replied, was the cutting edge
of abolitionism. Everything the abolitionists had accomplished dated from its first issue in January, 1831. "What
else," he asked, "but the *Liberator* primarily (and of
course instrumentally) has effected this change?"

The Tappans could be excused for failing to consider
the *Liberator* quite such a major factor in the abolitionist
movement. By 1833 it had about 1400 readers, fewer than
400 of them white, and annually ran $1700 in debt. Nei-
ther Garrison nor Knapp were careful businessmen, and
the paper's bookkeeping system was practically nonexistent. It carried appeals for funds in nearly every issue, and
Garrison made several trips to New York and Philadelphia in 1833 and 1834 to raise money. He asked the national society's executive committee to pay him an annual
salary, but they refused so long as the *Liberator* remained
outside their control. Next he and Knapp evolved a
scheme of selling shares in the paper at ten dollars each,
the money to be turned over to the New England society,

but the response was small. To make things worse, Garrison saddled the paper with a large investment in pamphlets, which he offered to sell to the national society. The society finally agreed to purchase part of the stock, and, with the gifts that trickled in, the *Liberator* continued somewhat shakily.

Garrison also had other and more personal reasons for wanting the *Liberator* to pay. In 1833, while visiting at the home of George Benson in Brooklyn, Connecticut, he met Benson's daughter Helen, a quiet, deeply religious girl of twenty-two. Her father, a friend of Lundy, was an oldtime antislavery man, and her two brothers, George and Henry, had both joined Garrison's New England society. Garrison and Helen became close friends, and after some months of visits and correspondence, she promised to marry him. Samuel May performed the ceremony at Brooklyn on September 4, 1834. After a short wedding trip Garrison rented a house at Roxbury, Massachusetts, near Boston, walking three miles to and from his office every day. His only income came from his agent's salary and the *Liberator*, neither of which furnished enough to support a wife and a prospective family with any security.

Garrison's position was not unique. No abolitionist in 1834 could look to the future with any optimism. Abolitionists, in New England and elsewhere, were not quite socially acceptable in respectable circles. In the opinion of William Ellery Channing, they stirred up "bitter passions and a fierce fanaticism." They did not, said the Reverend Horace Bushnell, "go to work like Christian gentlemen," nor did the clergy wholly approve of the *Liberator's* "denunciations, popular harangues . . . abhorrence, and hate." Henry Ware spoke to his fellow Unitarian May

about the "objectionable tone" of Garrison's paper, and
Emerson jotted in his journal: "The *Liberator* is a scold."
All Boston churches were closed to abolitionist meetings
except Phelps's and Channing's. Abolitionists tended
to be "queer," Bostonians noted; their meetings attracted
characters like "Father" Lamson, who grew a long white
beard, carried a scythe, and stood silently leaning on it
like Father Time, a symbol of mortality. Abby Folsom,
whose monomania was free speech, often broke up abolition gatherings by demanding the floor for her harangues, and even Garrison was unable to cope with her.
Once three men carried her bodily from an abolitionist
meeting, whereupon she remarked, "I'm better off than
Jesus — he had one ass to carry him, but I have three."

Boston's chief objection to Garrison was his language,
which, in the opinion of some abolitionists and all colonizationists, alienated the support of less aggressive and
more cultured antislavery sympathizers. Several members
of the national society's executive committee, wrote Lewis
Tappan, disapproved of Garrison's "harsh, unchristian vocabulary." The *Liberator*, said Birney, was the "fireship
in the abolition fleet." Hezekiah Niles, editor of *Niles'*
Register, believed Garrison "was doing all possible injury
to the cause of emancipation" and the Washington *Na-*
tional Intelligencer accused him of "poisoning the waters
of life to the whole community."

Garrison's answer to the charge that his attitude did
more harm than good to the antislavery cause was always
the same — the wicked must "be covered with thick in-
famy." "If those who deserve the lash feel it and wince at
it," he told May, "I shall be assured that I am striking the
right persons in the right place." With the *Liberator* as

his instrument, he hoped to rouse the public to such fury against slavery that the South would be forced to yield; harsh language alone could do it. It was impossible for any abolitionist to attack slavery "in good taste."

Garrison's vocabulary, sprinkled with "thief," "black-guard," "moral leper," "Satanic mansteraler," "degraded bully," and like terms, was a tool by which he tried to arouse powerful emotional reactions against slavery and slaveholders. His choicest epithets were usually reserved for his editorial opponents. Gales and Seaton of the hated *National Intelligencer* were "proverbially dull men, scurrilous and malignant." Colonel James Watson Webb's New York *Courier and Enquirer* was edited for and by "rum drinkers, lechers, pimps, and knaves." Another editor, mercifully left nameless, was "an irresponsible libeller, a shameless bastard, and a miserable craven." In width and variety, Garrison's invective was matched during the era probably only by that of James Gordon Bennett of the New York *Herald*. But the fact was that Garrison was a professional journalist, trained in the contemporary tradition of violence and abuse, writing at a time when canings and horsewhippings were not uncommon in editorial circles. Political journalism since the turn of the century had been marked by bad taste, vilification, and abuse. A vocabulary of epithets was standard journalistic equipment, and the most offensive Garrisonian phrases could have been easily matched in any of the partisan press since the Jeffersonian-Federalist battles of thirty years before. It was Garrison the editor, not Garrison the person, who lashed about him. Wendell Phillips, who knew him intimately for thirty years, never noted a single sentence in his conversation that reflected poor taste, nor did his children ever recall a hurtful phrase or a raised voice in the home.

Garrison seemed to thrive on opposition. By the mid-1830's he had gathered about him in Boston and New England a fanatically loyal band of followers. His sincerity and earnestness drew people to him, Lydia Maria Child said, "by pulling on the strings of conscience." Even those, like Emerson, who could not agree with his methods or his language admitted that there was in him "no falsehood or patchwork, but sincerity and unity." Those who followed him did so with utter devotion, considering him God's agent, another Moses or Elijah "raised up by Divine Providence," in Oliver Johnson's words, "to deliver this Republic from the sin and crime of slavery." Whenever he was attacked his supporters rushed to his aid. "It is resolved," read a typical resolution passed by the New England Antislavery Society in 1833, "that the course pursued by William Lloyd Garrison . . . has been and still is approved by us as the only true method of securing the rights and liberties of the colored people."

The nucleus of Garrison's Boston band was drawn equally from the ranks of radical reformers and fairly conservative professional people. Lewis Hayden, William Nell, and Charles Remond, all free Negroes, were intensely faithful to Garrison and spread his name in Negro circles. Oliver Johnson, who took over the *Liberator* in Garrison's absence, was a Vermonter whose *Christian Soldier,* an anti-Universalist paper, was founded in Boston simultaneously with the *Liberator.* George Benson (Garrison's father-in-law), Arnold Buffum, Joseph Southwick, and Joshua Coffin were all Quakers. Amos Phelps, George Cheever, and Samuel May were ministers, Phelps and

Cheever Congregationalists, the faithful May a Unitarian. Charles C. Follen was a Doctor of Laws from Jena, one-time soldier against Napoleon, refugee from Austria, pro-tégé of Lafayette, and Harvard professor of German; his death in 1840 in a steamboat explosion was a severe loss to the Boston circle. David Lee Child and Moses Thacher were editors of small Boston papers. Lydia Maria Child, David's wife, was a well-known writer of children's books and the author of an effective pamphlet called *An Appeal for the Class of Americans Called Africans*. Maria Chapman, wife of Henry G. Chapman, a prosperous merchant, was the mainstay of the Boston Female Antislavery Society, and both her husband and father-in-law were loyal Garri-sonians.

Wright, Burleigh, Foster, and Pillsbury came from a different social stratum. Henry C. Wright, a hatmaker who once studied theology, joined Garrison in 1835. A thoroughgoing radical, he was hired as an agent by the American Antislavery Society and created so much dis-turbance in New England that the Society finally trans-ferred him to Pennsylvania. Charles C. Burleigh was Ar-thur Tappan's discovery. As a law student in Connecticut, Burleigh came to the aid of Prudence Crandall and was hired by Tappan to edit the *Unionist,* a short-lived paper dedicated to her support. After moving to Boston he joined the New England Society and became one of its best rough-and-tumble debaters. He also grew a beard, long hair, and cultivated a resemblance to paintings of Christ that was especially effective with revivalist groups. Stephen S. Foster and Parker Pillsbury, young theology students, specialized in "abolitionizing" churches by the somewhat spectacular means of forcing their way into congregations and demanding to be heard from the pews. As a result they spent several sentences in jail as disturbers of the peace. Foster counted not only abolition, but peace, temperance, women's rights, labor unions, and abstinence from tobacco among his reforms; his book, *The Brotherhood of Thieves,* published in 1844, was the most vituperative attack on the clergy to appear in the period. He was so often accused of outright lunacy that the *Liberator,* to prove his sanity, once published the results of an examination of his skull by the famed phrenologist O. B. Fowler.

On the other hand, Francis Jackson, Samuel Sewall, Ellis Gray Loring, and Amasa Walker, Garrisonians all, came from Boston's upper crust. Jackson, Sewall, and Loring were prosperous lawyers, Walker a successful businessman. The only wealthy men in the group, they contributed heavily to the society and kept the *Liberator* alive for its first ten years. Their alliance with Foster, Wright, Pillsbury, and the rest was uneasy, and only respect for Garrison held them in the movement.

The New York abolitionists had their own troubles. That "Tappan and company" chose the city as the headquarters of the national antislavery society greatly embarrassed New York's merchants. Some business firms inserted notices in newspapers to assure Southern customers that they had no sympathy for abolitionists and frowned on "incendiary activities and publications." Prominent New Yorkers vowed "to frustrate and defeat the mischievous schemes of designing demagogues and deluded fanatics," while the city's newspapers, almost without exception, reported abolitionist activity with horror and scorn. In July,

1834, a mob sacked Lewis Tappan's home, wrecked two churches, and destroyed several houses in the Negro section. Mayor Lawrence called out the militia and deputized citizens to restore order, but it took three days for the riots to subside. The mayor blamed the American Antislavery Society, and Hezekiah Niles, in his *Register*, wrote that the riots were caused by "those foolish and dangerous men . . . who contend for the immediate emancipation of slaves and affect to desire an amalgamation between the whites and the blacks." Tappan protested that the abolitionists had "no desire to promote or encourage intermarriage . . . to dissolve the Union, or to violate the Constitution," but public opinion sided with Niles.

Garrison thought the New York riots a healthy sign. Abolitionism, if it provoked such powerful reactions, must be gaining ground. He opened a new column in the *Liberator,* "The Refuge of Oppression," to report cases of persecution and mob violence, and wrote almost hopefully of the fact that "some of us will be assassinated or abducted, seems more than probable."

The arrival of George Thompson from England, at Garrison's invitation, helped to create further disturbance. Thompson came in September, heralded by attacks in the Boston and New York press. "Another apostle of fanaticism," remarked the *Courier and Enquirer,* "hired by the immediate abolitionists to come among us and disseminate those precious doctrines of social equality and physical amalgamation." "Every slaveholder," the papers quoted Thompson, "ought to have his throat cut, and slaves ought to be taught how to cut them." (Thompson denied the statement, which was subsequently traced to an Andover theological student.) Under Garrison's sponsorship

Thompson toured New England, leaving a trail of disorder, mobs, and abuse behind him. The press termed him "A British emissary . . . the paid agent of the enemies of republican institutions," and ministers such as Henry Ware thought he "had no business in this country stirring up trouble."

While Thompson worked his way through New England, Tappan's students at Lane Seminary in the West found a practical method of putting Charles Finney's doctrine of "Christian usefulness" into operation. Theodore Weld and a group of abolitionist students promoted a series of debates in February, 1834, on the question of "*Immediatism* versus *Gradualism*." Gradualism lost, and with their eyes opened to "the specious exterior" of the colonization scheme the students voted to form an abolition society of their own. "Ohio will give no countenance to the followers of Garrison and Tappan," warned the Cincinnati *Gazette,* and public opinion finally forced the Lane Board of Trustees to outlaw student discussion of slavery, dissolve the student society, and forbid meetings for purposes "other than study or devotion." The board's action received wide publicity in the East and provided a topic for hundreds of Sunday sermons. Forty students immediately withdrew, most of them enrolling at Oberlin College in northern Ohio, which soon became the western center of abolition. Weld accepted a post as agent for the American Antislavery Society and organized a string of antislavery societies in Ohio.

In 1834 and 1835 the national society in New York found itself in trouble too, after it embarked on a pamphlet campaign to "awaken the conscience of the nation to the evils of slavery." The executive committee set aside a fund of $30,000 for the publication of a different periodical for each week of the month — a folio paper, *Human Rights;* a magazine, the *Antislavery Record;* a journal, the *Emancipator,* and a juvenile, the *Slave's Friend.* Distribution was by mail to names drawn from newspapers, organizational membership lists, and public records. Congressmen, ministers, legislators, lawyers, justices of the peace, and prominent citizens in all states received copies of the society's publications free of charge. In three years the society mailed out nearly two million pieces of literature.

Southern reaction to these indiscriminate mailings was swift, for the South remembered Nat Turner, the *Liberator,* and November, 1831, all too well. In Charleston a citizen's committee forced open the post office in July of 1835, removed packages of the society's publications, and burned them. In the rest of the South mass meetings urged postmasters "to detain and destroy all abolition papers." Several prominent Southerners, believing that some control of the mails ought to be established by law, appealed to Postmaster General Kendall. Kendall deftly sidestepped the issue, declaring that while he had no authority to exclude abolitionist pamphlets from the mails, neither could he direct postmasters to deliver them to addressees. Northern newspapers, sensitive to the threat of censorship, criticized Kendall's decision; at the same time, they agreed that indiscriminate mailings of "inflammatory propaganda" needed some supervision.

The national society replied that it had no intention of inciting revolt, that it sent nothing to slaves (who received no mail and who usually could not read), and that it sent nothing of an inflammatory nature to anybody. The charge against the society, of incendiarism, was more imaginary than real. Yet it was widely accepted in the South. As an Alabama lawyer remarked in 1835, "The antislavery societies . . . are doing all they can to destroy our domestic harmony by sending among us pamphlets, tracts, and newspapers for the purpose of exciting dissatisfaction and insurrection among our slaves." The American Colonization Society, quick to seize the opportunity, agreed that the aim of the Tappan group was "beyond a doubt, to foment a servile war in the South."

The controversy over the mails made the Northern public acutely conscious of the abolitionists. Most citizens lumped Garrison, the New Yorkers, and the Western group into the same category; all were "irresponsible agitators" who "threatened the harmony of society" and "undermined the government of our sister states." Disorder, division, and disharmony seemed to follow abolitionists wherever they went. To many antislavery sympathizers in Boston, Garrison's *Liberator* was a distinct liability, since it aroused tempers and irritated powerful elements in the community. In spring of 1834, therefore, a group of ministers, mostly Congregationalists with a sprinkling of Unitarians, decided to attempt to wrest the leadership of the antislavery movement in New England from Garrison's hands.

The ministers issued a call for a meeting to be held in January, 1835, to form a new society, the American Union for the Relief and Improvement of the Colored Race. Its principle, the announcement stated, was to be "that the system of slavery is wrong, and ought to be abandoned with the least possible delay"—a position designed to appeal to immediatist, gradualist, and colonizationist alike.

The group was, as Garrison correctly surmised, "an ANTI-GARRISON SOCIETY," and he blasted it in the *Liberator* as "a soulless organization with a sounding title." Garrison, Phelps, Loring, and Thompson attended the organizational meeting ready to debate, but got no chance. Arthur Tappan, much to Garrison's perturbation, came to talk to the officers of the Union and returned to New York to say that he could see no reason why the two societies might not profitably exist together. Arthur gave five thousand dollars to the Union's treasury, but Lewis refused to support it, predicting that it had little chance of survival. Lewis was right, for the Union collapsed within a year.

The American Union, even though it failed, reflected mounting opposition to Garrison. Although his New England society had only tenuous connections with the national society in New York, the hubbub over the mails centered Boston's attention on Garrison and his *Liberator*, while his constant attacks on local colonizationists angered the ministry.

In mid-1835 some fifteen hundred Bostonians signed a call for a public meeting, to be held in August, to explore the whole question of abolitionist agitation, and on August 21, with Mayor Theodore Lyman presiding, the meeting opened at Faneuil Hall. The preliminary resolutions accused the abolitionists of attempting to "scatter among our Southern friends firebrands, arrows, and death," and indignantly denounced "the intrusion upon our domestic relations of foreign emissaries" — an obvious reference to George Thompson. Harrison Gray Otis, Garrison's one-time Federalist idol, Peleg Sprague, Senator from Massachusetts, Richard Fletcher, a prominent local lawyer, and others spoke, decrying agitation and appealing for com-

mon sense and unity. Garrison retorted the next day that
Faneuil Hall, once the Cradle of Liberty, should now be
renamed "The Refuge of Slavery," since it had been
"turned into an Augean stable by proslavery apologists."
Mayor Lyman, worried at the temper of the exchange, quietly advised Garrison that it would be wise to postpone
meetings of his society until public opinion cooled.

Garrison paid no attention to Lyman's advice. Feeling
against Thompson, who had spent nearly a year in New
England, ran high. When he announced his return to
Boston in October, there were mutterings that "Garrison
and Thompson and their associates ought to be put down."
The New England Antislavery Society engaged Congress
(formerly Julien) Hall for Thompson's lecture, but the
owner, fearing trouble, withdrew his permission. The lecture, the *Liberator* announced, would be given later at
another date and another place, but the Boston Female
Antislavery Society would hold its regular meeting in the
society's Hall at 46 Washington Street. Though no talk by
Thompson was advertised, the rumor spread that he
would arrive on October twenty-first to address the Female
Society. A placard appeared in the streets, announcing that
since "the infamous foreign scoundrel . . . would be in
town," Boston's citizenry would have an "opportunity to
snake him out to a tar kettle."

The ladies' meeting was scheduled for three o'clock in
the afternoon. When Garrison arrived at the offices at two-
thirty, he found nearly a hundred people milling about
the entrance and about twenty frightened women huddled
in the hall inside. He went to his own office, where C. C.
Burleigh was already at his desk. While the two
men talked quietly they heard shouts outside; at three

o'clock the crowd, Garrison estimated, numbered nearly a thousand. Promptly on the hour a group of men entered the hall, interrupted the ladies' meeting, and began a search for Thompson. Mayor Lyman, hearing the confusion, arrived with the sheriff, and advised the crowd to go home since Thompson was not there. When the crowd showed no sign of retiring, Lyman asked the ladies to leave, which they did — resuming their meeting at Maria Chapman's home a few blocks away. While Lyman talked to the crowd, the group of men inside the building crashed into Garrison's office, exclaiming, "That's Garrison, that's the scoundrel!" but the sheriff ordered them out. Lyman proposed that Garrison leave by a rear window to avoid further trouble. Garrison did so, and the sheriff announced to the crowd that he had gone.

Some sharp-eyed men on the crowd's outskirts, however, saw Garrison escape and followed him to a carpenter's shop, where he lay hidden in a second-floor room. The shouting mob followed. His pursuers searched him out, caught him, and tied a rope around his waist; then, in full view of the crowd, Garrison climbed out the window and down a ladder to the street. Burleigh, back at the society offices, heard a cry, "They've got him!" and feared the worst, but the men who seized him when he reached the street were probably Lyman's men. They fended off the crowd — crying "Don't hurt him! He is an American!" — and took him safely through the mob to City Hall. Lyman, advising Garrison that it was best for his safety, booked him for disturbing the peace and apologetically placed him in a hack, ringed by the sheriff's deputies, bound for city jail. The mob followed him to the jail and then dispersed.

Garrison was convinced his martyrdom had come. He

felt, he said later, perfectly calm and happy, believing it "indeed a blessed privilege thus to suffer for Christ." He rather enjoyed his night in jail, holding long conversations through the window with friends and occupying his time between callers by writing a long inscription on the wall:

William Lloyd Garrison was put into this jail on Wednesday afternoon, October 21, 1835, to save him from the violence of a "respectable and influential mob," who sought to destroy him for preaching the abominable and dangerous doctrine that "all men are created equal" and that all oppression is odious in the sight of God.

The next morning Mayor Lyman held a brief examination in Garrison's cell, dismissed the charge and released him. On Lyman's advice Garrison decided to leave town for a few days, and Sheriff Parkman drove him to Canton, where he met his wife and journeyed to Providence for a vacation. On November 7 he was back in Boston, doing business at the *Liberator* offices again. George Thompson, who arrived after the trouble was over, kept out of sight until he sailed for England a week later. The majority of the newspapers in Boston and elsewhere, whatever their initial responsibility for the mob, decried the use of violence and pointed out the threat to free speech involved. Some responsibility, said the Boston *Transcript*, nevertheless rested on the abolitionists themselves and particularly on Garrison. "We cannot but deplore," the editorial continued, "that our city should be the stage for such tumultuous scenes — but in what terms of indignation can we speak of the man, who by his rancorous denunciations, and his brawling, ferocious abuse, together with the disorganizing tendency of his doctrines, has excited the people to such an ebullition of their deeply exasperated feelings?"

There was never any real trouble for the *Liberator* in Boston again, although both Garrison and Knapp constantly spoke of an impending attack on its offices, and expected one. Garrison was ready. "The truth that we utter," he wrote, "is impalpable yet real; it cannot be thrust down by brute force, nor pierced with a dagger, nor bribed with gold, nor overcome by the application of tar and feathers."

I V

We Have Made Clean Work

BY THE MID-1830's the "conspiracy of silence" had been broken. Whether people liked it or not slavery was a topic for open discussion; the issue of freedom for the slave could never be suppressed again. But the implications of their own demands confused the abolitionists. Was theirs a religious or a political movement? That slavery was a moral evil they could all agree. But by what machinery could it be most swiftly eliminated?

To the rank and file of the abolitionists the most effective way to strike directly at slavery was through united political action. There was very little chance, as realistic antislavery leaders knew, of ever achieving an antislavery majority in the slave states. The national government, however, had authority to end slavery in any state by Federal law. Wherever one looked, the road to success pointed toward Washington. Therefore abolition, much against Garrison's will, inevitably became involved in politics.

The task of organizing proceeded fairly well. In the West, Theodore Weld trained thirteen of the young Lane rebels as Antislavery Society agents, and he himself toured Ohio, western Pennsylvania, and New York State, leaving behind a string of new societies. Henry B. Stanton, another Lane student, took Rhode Island and Connecticut as his territory. James G. Birney, discouraged in his attempt to abolitionize Kentucky, moved to Cincinnati, founded the *Philanthropist,* and helped to establish the Ohio Antislavery Society. In 1837 the national society listed 1,006 affiliated societies, local, state, and regional. That same year the society reorganized itself, put full-time secretaries in charge of the New York office, and left the Tappans as more or less honorary directors. Birney came East to head the executive committee, Stanton handled finances, Leavitt replaced Goodell on the *Emancipator,* Wright remained as executive secretary. Anticipating an expanded organizational campaign, the committee hired Weld to train seventy more agents, nearly half of them former Lane students.

By the end of the decade there were several well-defined clusters of abolitionist activity in the North. The American Antislavery Society represented a union of New York City, Pennsylvania, and Western groups, based on "the Lane-New York principle" of immediatism. In upper New York State, where the State Society was dominant, another group led by Gerrit Smith, Alvan Stewart, Myron Holley, and William Jay, worked in harmony with the national organization. The peripatetic Goodell, after leaving the *Emancipator,* founded and edited the state society's organ, the *Friend of Man.* In the Philadelphia area the old Pennsylvania society kept up an independent existence, loosely connected with the national society.

For all practical purposes, abolitionism in New England existed by itself. Only one fifth of the names on the American Antislavery Society's membership rolls came from

New England; here Garrison's New England Antislavery Society (which changed its name to the Massachusetts Antislavery Society in 1836) was in control. Its agents sold the *Liberator*, organized societies in the smaller towns, and saw to it that delegates to the annual New England Antislavery Convention followed Garrison's lead. Though the New England society contributed annually to the American Antislavery Society's treasury, its connections with the New York executive committee were vague. In New England only one abolitionist group seemed to exist outside the Garrisonian framework. After one branch of the Methodist church adopted its own modified version of immediatism, Orange Scott and La Roy Sunderland organized a Methodist society and founded *Zion's Watchman* as its organ.

Abolitionist societies, whatever their nature, faced hostility everywhere. Few people then saw any reason to agitate the slavery question unduly, and even fewer approved of the abolitionists' methods of agitating it. The Reverend Elijah Barrows, writing in 1836, summarized the charges against them: first, they incited slave revolts; second, they undermined Southern prosperity; third, they promoted disunity among the states; fourth, they disturbed the peace and order of society; and last, they worsened the Negroes' lot by irritating the feelings of slaveholders. The anonymous author of *The South Vindicated from the Treason and Fanaticism of the Abolitionists* also accused them of encouraging religious infidelity, of attacking the Constitution, and of advocating racial amalgamation — this last a charge that appeared and reappeared in anti-abolitionist literature for thirty years. Calvin Colton, in his widely distributed pamphlet *Abolition a Sedition,* believed that abolitionism "endangered racial purity"; James Buchanan of Pennsylvania spoke of the "disgusting scenes" that would follow emancipation; abolitionist publications, it was rumored, printed cuts of Negroes and whites in compromising positions. At Zanesville, Ohio, placards posted before an abolitionist lecture urged townspeople to break up the meeting in order "to rid ourselves of the disgrace of racial amalgamation."

Nearly all the antiabolitionist publications agreed that the most serious charge against the abolitionists was that they disturbed the peace and harmony of society. Their doctrines, said Newark, New Jersey's *Sentinel of Freedom,* stirred up riots, discouraged moderation, and prevented dispassionate consideration of the whole slavery question. Their "ill manners," said the Reverend Horace Bushnell, damaged the reputations of reasonable reformers and checked the progress of antislavery in the South. "Exasperating the master," remarked Governor Edward Everett of Massachusetts, only rendered "more oppressive the condition of the slave." The Reverend William Ellery Channing pleaded for antislavery argument that was "calm, general, and unmixed with personalities," while the Reverend Leonard Bacon took Garrison to task, as many did, for his "intemperate attacks" on men of good will. "Agitation of the question of immediate emancipation," a public meeting decided in Lowell, Massachusetts, "is calculated to create disaffection and suspicion . . ." and Abraham Lincoln, serving in the Illinois legislature in 1837, signed a memorandum to the effect that while slavery was "both injustice and bad policy," the "promulgation of abolition doctrines tends rather to increase than to abate its evils."

Northern businessmen saw in abolitionist activity a particular danger to trade with the South, whose merchants frequently threatened to boycott the "abolitionist nests" of Boston and New York. One New York businessman frankly told Samuel May, "There are millions and millions of dollars which would be jeopardized by any rupture between North and South. We cannot afford, sir, to let you and your associates succeed in your endeavor to overthrow slavery." In the same vein Mayor Harrison Gray Otis of Boston assured the South that New England approved of only those antislavery societies that made "temperate appeals to reason and the principles of humanity, [such] as are consistent with the peace and safety and rights and necessities of the state of society of our Southern brethren." Hezekiah Niles no doubt spoke for the majority when he reported in his *Register* in 1836 that most Northerners "considered slavery a great moral and national evil and wish that it were removed; but . . . they unanimously believe that there is no right in the general government to interfere with the plantation states in the management of their own slaves."

Much of the opposition the abolitionists encountered in the North sprang from a general misunderstanding of the principle of *immediate* emancipation. The immediatists, as distinguished from gradualists and colonizationists, agreed that slavery should be abolished at once; but they were unable to agree on how, or why. Failure to find a satisfactory definition of their own term caused internal dissension within abolitionist circles and aroused opposition from without. "Immediate" meant to the public at large exactly what it said; the Negro slave was to be freed at once, thrown on the community with full civil, economic, and social rights. "Immediate and complete emancipation," said Leonard Bacon (next to Beecher the most powerful Congregationalist clergyman in New England) can be "construed only in the obvious meaning of the term. Hence the call for an immediate abolitionist meeting is so often the signal for some demonstration of popular indignation." The whole principle of immediatism, agreed William Ellery Channing, "almost certainly conveys a wrong sense and needs explanation."

The abolitionists wrestled manfully with the problem of explaining it. The New York City society, at the time of its founding in 1832, adopted British doctrine *in toto*. Labeling themselves "immediatists," the Tappans explained, simply meant that they did not believe in "the project of gradual emancipation which had failed to work" in the West Indies. Still following British precedent, the New York committee evolved a doctrine of "immediate emancipation, gradually accomplished" by freeing the slave but holding him under "necessary restraint" until he was prepared to assume his responsibilities in a free society. That position was easily misunderstood, and the American Antislavery Society, which adopted the city society's principle, instructed its agents to avoid lengthy discussions of it. "Let the *principle* be decided on, of immediate abolition," wrote Lewis Tappan, "and the plans will easily present themselves."

The Lane rebels added a variation of their own. If slavery was sinful, it must not be tolerated for an instant; it must be immediately abolished — and how could eliminating a sin bring anything but good? Thus they shifted the ground of the debate to theology, opening a decade of

"Bible argument" that produced dozens of pamphlets proving that the Bible either did, or did not, condone slavery. By making abolition a religious issue, the Lane group established a much more tenable basis for immediatism. The extirpation of slavery, said the Lane society's constitution, must be accomplished "not by rebellion, war, or congressional interference." Rather the slaveholders must be convinced of the sin of slavery "through the presentation of fact and argument, and appealing to their hearts and minds" — and this work must begin immediately. "By immediate emancipation," the Lane men explained, "we do not mean that the slaves shall be turned loose on the nation." Their goal, rather, was "gradual emancipation, immediately begun." The master's control over the Negro was to cease at once; the freedman was to be employed as a laborer but "placed under a benevolent and disinterested supervision . . . until ready for intellectual and moral equality with whites."

The Lane doctrine proved somewhat more palatable to the majority of abolitionists than the original New York principle, and soon was combined with it. After the publication of Thome and Kimball's study, *Emancipation in the West Indies* — which seemed to show that such a transition from slave to free labor had worked well under British auspices — the Lane-New York doctrine became the most widely accepted version of immediatism. As John Greenleaf Whittier's pamphlet *Justice and Expediency* explained, no abolitionist really expected that "the tremendous system of oppression can instantaneously be overthrown." But, Whittier concluded, *agitation* against it could and must begin at once. Arthur Tappan was so struck by the clarity and effectiveness of Whittier's argument that he purchased and distributed five thousand copies of the pamphlet.

Garrison, except for the early years of his career, was not greatly concerned about delicate nuances of definition. In January, 1832, he explained that there were three methods by which slavery might be abolished: first, by physical force; second, by slave revolt; and third, by appealing to "an enlightened and benevolent public opinion." The first two methods were obviously unacceptable.

Having thus defined the method, he explained his aims. "By immediate emancipation," he wrote in December, 1832, "we do not mean

> That the slaves shall be turned loose upon the nation, to roam as vagabonds or aliens, — nor
> That they shall be instantly invested with all political rights and privileges, — nor
> That they shall be expelled from their native land to a foreign clime, as the price and condition of their freedom.

"But we mean" — he continued —

> That instead of being under the unlimited control of a few irresponsible masters, they shall really receive the protection of the law;
> That the power which is now vested in every slaveholder . . . shall instantly cease;
> That the slaves shall be employed as free laborers, fairly compensated, and protected in their earnings;
> That they shall be placed under a benevolent and disinterested supervision, which shall secure to them the right to obtain secular and religious knowledge, to worship God according to the dictates of their own consciences, to accumulate wealth, and to seek intellectual and moral mastery over their white competitors.

In January, of 1836, he placed the same passage at the masthead of the *Liberator*. With a few changes, it remained there for some years; the words "mastery" and "competitors" in the last sentence were dropped, "equality" and "brethren" substituted. The matter of granting votes to freed Negroes, however, bothered Garrison. In the first issue of the *Liberator* he proclaimed, "I shall strenuously contend for the immediate enfranchisement for the slave population." A year later, however, in *Thoughts on African Colonization,* he explained, "Immediate abolition does not mean that slaves shall immediately exercise the right of suffrage or be eligible for any office . . . We contend for the immediate *personal* freedom of slaves."

Samuel May, who worked closely with him for thirty years, always claimed that Garrison's aim was grossly misconstrued. "Our only demand," he wrote, "for our enslaved countrymen has been that they should forthwith be admitted to all the rights and privileges of freemen upon the same condition as others, after they shall have acquired (those of them who do not now possess) the qualifications demanded of others." Amos Phelps, whose *Lectures on Slavery and Its Remedy* appeared in 1834, almost certainly with Garrison's approval, defined immediatism as "simply that the slaves be at once delivered from the control of arbitrary and irresponsible power, and like other men, put under the control of equitable laws equitably administered." In effect, the Garrisonian principle closely followed the British and the Lane New York doctrines of immediate beginnings leading to carefully qualified ends.

The fine distinctions of immediatist doctrine were for the most part lost on the public. Through the 1830's and 1840's attacks on abolitionists poured from the press, mass meetings passed anti-abolitionist resolutions, and clergy-men censured them. Garrison's intemperate language and his uncompromising aggressiveness, it was assumed, rep-resented immediate abolitionism; no matter how many carefully-worded disclaimers came from the national and state societies, the public tended to see the issue in Garri-sonian terms, and to see in it only agitation, revolt, social upheaval, disunion, and miscegenation. There was no question of what the South saw. "Let the hell-hounds of the North beware," warned the Richmond *Whig,* and it was rumored in Boston that some Southerner had offered three thousand dollars for Garrison's ears. Opposition grew in the North, too. Threatening letters came almost daily to the New York office of the American Antislavery Society, and its agents, working through New England, New York, and the West, found mobs waiting for them. Abolition lec-turers took to wearing "storm suits" of old clothes, the better to withstand barrages of eggs and vegetables, and the *Antislavery Record* published "Hints on Abolition Mobs" with instructions to its agents.

During 1835 and 1836, the "mob years," abolitionists claimed to have been involved in three hundred riots, al-though their count was likely to lump minor disturbances with more serious attacks. Most "mobocrats," wrote Thur-low Weed, an Ohio agent, "seldom do anything but make swelling threats," but abolition speakers were often sub-jected to indignity and rudeness. Throwing eggs, ink, or paint, placing red pepper or asafetida in the meetinghouse stove, drowning out the speaker with catcalls or horns, blockading the building in which the meeting was to be held — these were common methods of dispersing aboli-tionist meetings. A few men were roughly handled, espe-

cially after the national society sent out its famous seventy
agents; Marius Robinson nearly died at the hands of an
Ohio mob, and Weld suffered a concussion from a thrown
brick. The worst areas, agents agreed, were New York
City, upper New York State, and eastern Ohio. New England mobs tended to be vocal rather than physically dangerous.

Mobs were usually an indication, abolitionists believed,
that abolitionism was gaining ground in a community.
"Every abolition lecture they break up," the *Record*
pointed out, "is a ruinous victory to the cause of slavery,"
since respectable men would soon realize that stifling abolitionist talk endangered freedom of speech and assembly.
In seizing on the issue of free speech versus mob law, the
abolitionists hoped to turn their opposition into an asset.
"Mob disturbances," wrote Catherine Beecher, were "generally spoken of with exultation by Abolitionists, as . . .
among the chief means of promoting their cause. How
many men have declared or implied, that in joining the
ranks of Abolition, they were influenced not by their arguments, but because the violence of opposers had identified
that course with the question of free speech, freedom of
the press, and civil liberty?"

The abolitionists succeeded in identifying their cause
with the rights of free speech and press. Though the *Liberator,* the *Emancipator,* the *Friend of Man,* and other papers had small circulations in the North and practically
none in the South, it was common to assign to them "mur-
derous designs" for fomenting slave revolts. After 1831,
with the unfortunate juxtaposition of Nat Turner and the
Liberator, states in the lower South looked suspiciously at
Northern publications and watched their own carefully.

Virginia, Maryland, Georgia, North Carolina, and South Carolina passed new laws governing the press or tightened old ones; Mississippi, Alabama, and Tennessee followed the pattern established by the seaboard states. As a Southern mass meeting in 1835 resolved, "Freedom of speech and press does not imply a moral right to freely discuss the subject of slavery . . . , a question too nearly allied to the vital interests of the slave holding states to admit of public disputation." Still, it was not the frightening language of the laws, but public opinion that kept the Southern press free of antislavery taint. Southern editors with antislavery leanings were usually discouraged by social and economic pressure long before their views reached the prosecution stage. Antislavery sympathizers learned to keep quiet and not to subscribe to Northern papers.

The life of an abolitionist editor in the North was not easy. A substantial number of the riots reported in abolitionist papers involved antislavery editors, the most conspicuous being the Boston mob of 1835 that nearly caught Garrison, the Cincinnati mob of 1836 over Birney's *Philanthropist,* and most important, the Illinois mob of 1837 that killed Elijah Lovejoy, editor of the Alton *Observer.* Pressure came from the South to bar abolitionist publications from the mails, or to prosecute abolitionist editors for disturbing the peace. The legislatures of South Carolina, Virginia, Georgia, and Alabama transmitted memorials to the legislatures of ten Northern states in 1836, asking that it be made a penal offense "to print, publish, and distribute newspapers, tracts, and pictorial representations, calculated and having an obvious tendency to excite the slaves of the slave states to insurrection and revolt." Definition of what constituted an "obvious tendency" was left

vague, and most Northern editors, sensitive to infringe-
ments on freedom of the press, gave the memorials a cold
reception. Major urban newspapers, such as the New York
Sun and the *Evening Post*, the Boston *Courier*, and the
Cincinnati *Gazette*, warned that the legislation requested
by the South endangered editorial freedom everywhere,
however desirable it might be to curb the abolitionists.
Small papers, such as the Piqua, Ohio, *Western Courier*
and the Greensburgh, Iowa, *Repository*, thought that the
abolitionist must "be protected in his full exercise of freedom" even though one disagreed with his views. At the
same time a substantial number of editors, particularly in
the abolitionist centers of New York and Boston, hoped
that some other way might be found to prevent Garrison
and his brethren from "sowing seeds of discord in our communities."

The abolitionists seized on the issue at once. "Let them
press laws abridging our freedom of speech," said Elizur
Wright — "so much the better." If the continued existence
of slavery meant denial of freedom of press and speech in
North and South, the editor who attacked slavery was,
quite logically, the defender and protector of that freedom
— and he lost no time in proclaiming that he was. "Abolitionists may be the first victims of arbitrary power," the
American Antislavery Society warned, "but not the last."

The murder of Elijah Lovejoy gave the abolitionists a
magnificent opportunity to plead their case. Boston's reaction was typical. When the news of the Alton tragedy
reached the city, a committee of one hundred prominent
citizens, headed by William Ellery Channing, called a mass
meeting of protest in Faneuil Hall. Neither Garrison nor

his antislavery society had any connection with the call, nor did he speak at the meeting. But the meeting itself marked the first public appearance of Wendell Phillips, whose speech in defense of Lovejoy became a minor oratorical classic, and who immediately joined Garrison's society to become the most powerful orator in the abolitionist movement. Edmund Quincy, the son of Harvard's great President Josiah Quincy, joined Garrison at almost the same time. Both were valuable acquisitions; wealthy and aristocratic young men, they represented support of a class hitherto untouched by Garrisonism.

Many others felt as Phillips and Quincy did, for Lovejoy's death rocked the entire North. It gave "a shock as of any earthquake throughout this continent," wrote John Quincy Adams, and after 1837 abolitionism and freedom of the press merged into a single cause. William Cullen Bryant's *Evening Post* regarded the issue as one of freedom versus "despotism and anarchy"; Horace Greeley in the *New Yorker* considered Lovejoy "a martyr to public liberty." The *Emancipator* reprinted one hundred and sixty-one editorials from both Northern and Southern newspapers, all of them condemning the mob, and Garrison reprinted fifty. The Alton mob ended forever any legislative threat to the abolitionist press. Because of that threat, Henry Wilson wrote later in his history of the antislavery movement, "large accessions were made to the ranks of pronounced and avowed abolitionists."

The Massachusetts State Legislature received the Southern memorials cordially. The incumbent Whig party favored antiabolitionist legislation and had the votes to pass it. Since Boston was the home of Garrison and the *Liberator,* Massachusetts was acutely aware of the abolitionists in its midst; Governor Everett had already pointed out that anything "calculated to excite revolt and insurrection among the slaves" could be prosecuted as a misdemeanor at common law. With an implied recommendation that something be done, he referred the matter to a five-men legislative committee headed by Senator George Lunt of Newburyport, Garrison's birthplace.

Samuel May, secretary of the Massachusetts Antislavery Society, asked the Lunt Committee for a hearing — not to defend abolitionism, he explained, which needed no defense, but "to avert any action of the Legislature that might infringe the liberty of speech, or of the press." On March 4 Garrison, May, Loring, Sewall, Southwick, Follen, Jackson, and Goodell appeared before the committee. Garrison began by defending himself against charges of intending to destroy the Union. Follen, who spoke next, began a heated attack on the South and after several warnings Lunt cut him off, declaring the hearing dissolved on the ground that Follen's remarks were truculent and disrespectful.

The society protested Lunt's ruling, and on the eighth the committee agreed to meet the abolitionists again, this time in the House of Representatives before a large audience attracted by the publicity given the first hearing. May and Sewall argued the constitutional right of the abolitionists to free speech. Follen spoke more temperately than before. But William Goodell threw the hearing into an uproar by turning from a defense of the abolitionist press to a heated attack on the Southern "slave power" which, he charged, was deliberately attempting to "rob the free states of those liberties brought to Massachusetts by the Pilgrims and cherished by their descendants." The real question, Goodell cried, was "one of *liberty* and *rights* — not *black,* but *white* and *black!"* Lunt immediately closed the hearing and sent the abolitionists away, but their mission had been accomplished. When the Lunt Committee finally reported weeks later, it labeled the Garrisonians as "disunionists, agitators, visionaries and . . . enemies of peace and the Constitution," but it also failed to recommend any legislative action.

The *Liberator* hailed the report as a victory both for abolitionism and for freedom of the press, while Garrison reported that the Massachusetts society gained a number of new members after the hearings. All of the Northern legislatures eventually rejected the Southern appeals, limiting themselves like the Lunt Committee to pleas for calmness and temperance. The relationship between abolitionism and freedom of speech and press was too well established for them to do otherwise. The memory of "the martyr of Alton" was too powerful an argument to refute.

Though Garrison congratulated the Massachusetts society for its victory over the Lunt Committee, his position in the society was rapidly becoming less secure. He had a devoted band of followers, but to many of the rank-and-file members he seemed arrogant and dictatorial — "a whip-master-general," one of them said angrily. He brooked no rivals and tolerated little disagreement; he defined the terms of abolitionism and he enforced them. Then too the *Liberator* had begun to devote large amounts of space to strictures against cock-fighting, tobacco, liquors, war, and "infidelity," so much that to its readers it appeared that the abolition of Negro slavery seemed to be only one of its editor's aims, and at times a lesser one. That Garrison dealt rather shortly with mild criticisms of his editorial policy irritated those subscribers who simply wanted to read an antislavery paper. Those close to Garrison understood his propensity for reform — any reform — and knew also that to him no worthy cause was minor. The cockpit and the slave mart both were bad; true, one was much worse than the other, but Garrison could never see any logic in not fighting on several fronts at once.

To make matters worse, early in 1836 Garrison began correspondence with John Humphrey Noyes, who in founding his Perfectionist society two years before had included in it some interesting ideas on sex. All human institutions, Noyes believed, were obstacles to human progress; the only proper society was a Biblically-based anarchy in which perfect human beings acted wholly by inner law. Noyes' arguments (excepting those concerning domestic life) appealed to Garrison. Finally Garrison, who did nothing by halves, announced to his startled readers that he too, like Noyes, had decided to "reject all allegiance to his country" since all human governments were "anti-Christ." "Both church and state," he told the Providence Antislavery Society, were "corrupt" — both must "be dashed to pieces." Garrison's announcement shocked the Boston abolitionists, especially Sewall and Loring, who were both strong constitutionalists and well-trained lawyers. To others, "no-governmentism" smacked of anarchy, infidelity, and immorality. Few beyond Garrison's personal followers could perceive any relationship between Noyesian Perfectionism and abolition.

Affairs in Boston were further complicated by the appearance of the Grimké sisters, Angelina and Sarah, South Carolina Quakers who had been converted to immediate abolition in 1835. A year later the American Antislavery

Society appointed them as lecturers, after much discussion over the propriety of sponsoring female speakers, and they made a tremendously successful tour of women's antislavery auxiliaries in the New York City area. The Massachusetts Society invited them to Boston in 1837, and since Boston ladies frequently took husbands and male guests to their meetings, the Grimkés soon had predominantly male audiences. Remarks about the propriety of women speaking in public, particularly on controversial topics, led May, Whittier, and Phelps to remonstrate with Garrison, who had once felt so strongly about the place of women in reform organizations that he refused to accept female antislavery petitions to Congress.

"Carolina's high-souled daughters," however, were a huge success, and objections to their appearances before "promiscuous assemblies" immediately brought up the question of women's rights. Garrison urged the sisters to continue, the Massachusetts society arranged for Angelina to appear before legislative hearings, and for a time the Grimkés were figures of national prominence. Henry C. Wright took them over, planned their itinerary, wrote reports of their lectures for the *Liberator,* and counseled them; while Weld, who was personally interested in Angelina, worried over her ecstatic letters in praise of Garrison.

The introduction of the women's rights issue into the abolitionist argument displeased many. "The term Female Orator," said one minister, "has a sound too nearly allied to another that may not be named." Abolitionists who favored women's rights in the abstract hesitated to adopt them in practice. The cause of slavery, some complained, seemed to be disappearing in the cause of women's rights; raising the "woman question" simply muddied and diverted the whole antislavery argument. "Don't push your *women's* rights," Weld cautioned, "until *human* rights have gone ahead and broken the path," but Angelina and Sarah continued to draw huge audiences while Garrison applauded. Weld finally married Angelina, as another put it, to "save her from Garrison." Sarah, without her sister, took a less prominent role in the movement.

At the same time that Garrison involved himself with Noyes and the Grimkés, he began a running battle with the New England clergy. Garrison had hoped since his days with Lundy to enlist the clergy in the vanguard of the abolition movement. Since 1831 he had attempted vainly to persuade prominent clergymen in New England to join his cause, meeting for the most part only open hostility. Lyman Beecher, who thought that immediatists and colonizationists should cooperate in the common cause, convinced the New England Congregational Assembly in 1832 that a "union, blessed union" of antislavery forces was possible and desirable. After that Garrison's exhortations to the clergy fell on closed ears. His language offended prominent clergymen, such as Moses Stuart of Andover, Nathan Lord of Dartmouth, Bishop Hopkins of Vermont, and Leonard Bacon and Nehemiah Adams of Boston, all of whom regarded him as an irresponsible fanatic (possibly an agnostic) infected by Noyes, women's rights, and "no-government anarchism."

Garrison continued his overtures to the Church, but Beecher's influence was far too strong. In 1834 Amos Phelps, a Congregational minister himself, pleaded the case for immediatism before the Association of Congregational Ministers of Massachusetts, but he received a polite hearing and nothing more. When Garrison's own Baptist

Board of Foreign Missions refused to accept immediate emancipation, he gave up hope. The orthodox churches, he decided bitterly, were "disgraces to Christianity . . . heathenish, filled with apologies for sin and sinners of the worst sort . . . predominantly corrupt and servile." But one conclusion could be drawn. American Christianity was "the main pillar of American Slavery."

After 1835 Garrison's attacks on the church redoubled in violence. The Methodist Church was "a cage of unclean birds and a synagogue of Satan"; Congregational clerics were "implacable foes of God and man"; Presbyterians and Baptists were controlled by "blackhearted clergy" who connived with slaveholders." An "oath-taking, war-making, man-enslaving religion" passed as Christianity in New England, and the *Liberator* fulminated against it. The clergy quite understandably resented the attacks, and when Beecher suggested that the Congregational Association of Connecticut close its pulpits to "itinerant agents and lecturers" who preached "erroneous or questionable" sentiments, the Association unanimously approved. A few weeks later Beecher put a similar resolution through the Congregational Association of Massachusetts, shutting the doors of the most powerful church in New England to the abolitionists.

Garrison's war with the clergy filled the New York offices of the American Antislavery Society with dismay. Massachusetts and Connecticut appeared to be lost to the cause, and only a swift trip by Weld and Stanton to New Hampshire saved that state from Beecher. Garrison, in Lewis Tappan's opinion, was sowing "germs of animosity and contention among the brethren." But Garrison would hear nothing of compromise. Instead, he started a new fight with the clergy over the sanctity of the Sabbath. Although he had once refused to send or receive mail on Sunday lest he desecrate the day, he announced in the *Liberator* that "keeping the Sabbath as a holy day" was simply "an outworn and foolish superstition" that he intended to explode. Boston was shocked again. Goodell, May, and Phelps all remonstrated with him, and some of the abolitionist faithful began to lose faith, suspecting him of "a decided wish, nay a firm resolve, in laboring to overthrow slavery to overthrow the Christian Sabbath and the Christian ministry." "Still do I beg of you, brother," pleaded Elizur Wright from New York, "to let other subjects alone until slavery is finished."

The New England clergymen replied to Garrison in July, 1837. That month the General Association of Congregational Ministers of Massachusetts, meeting at West Brookfield, authorized distribution of a "pastoral Letter" to all Congregational Churches. Chiefly from the hand of the Reverend Nehemiah Adams (called derisively "Southside" Adams by Garrisonians because of his book, *A Southside View of Slavery*) the *Pastoral Letter* decried the "alienation and division" caused by discussions of "perplexed and agitating subjects" and advised both clergy and laity to avoid them. Women, the *Letter* continued, ought not to appear in public meetings, nor should they engage in "doubtful disputations." "Preachers or lecturers on certain topics of reform" should not be allowed "to present their subjects within the parochial limits of settled pastors without their consent." "The Brookfield Bull," as Garrison called it, dealt the Massachusetts Antislavery Society a body blow.

Oliver Johnson and Garrison retaliated in the *Liberator,*

singling out Adams and his co-authors as "blind leaders of
the blind, dumb dogs that cannot bark, spiritual popes"
deep in sin. "There is no malignity," he remarked, "like
that of a corrupt priest when he finds his mask of profession
fails to conceal his moral deformity." On August 2 five
Congregational ministers published another document,
"The Appeal of the Clerical Abolitionists on Antislavery
Measures," protesting both Garrison's language and his
"hasty insinuations" about respected clergymen. On August 3 the faculty of Andover Theological Seminary issued
a third document censuring the Garrisonians, and religious
newspapers, such as the *Christian Mirror,* the New York
Evangelist, and the New York *Observer,* joined in. Although Garrison, Johnson, and Phelps replied in kind, the
ecclesiastical artillery was too heavy for them. Garrison appealed to the executive committee of the American Antislavery Society for support, but Lewis Tappan, who said
he saw "too much truth in the charges," refused to give it.
A *Second Clerical Appeal,* circulated by the Congregational clergy in September, convinced a number of abolitionists that Garrison's propensity for creating powerful
enemies more than outweighed his usefulness to the antislavery cause.

Although Garrison pointed out that none of the signers
of the *Pastoral Letter* or of the two *Appeals* were "true
abolitionists," the board of the Massachusetts society felt
he had overreached himself in drawing down on them the
ire of the Congregational Church. The board therefore issued a statement denying that the society was "controlled
by any single person," and Garrison heard a rumor that the
society might have a new paper, completely divorced from

him and from the *Liberator*. If this was true, Garrison was finished as an effective abolitionist leader.

The American Antislavery Society in New York announced that the public should not "confound their doctrines with such as individual members may occasionally advance" and sent Birney to New England to survey the situation. Birney's report was not optimistic. "I greatly lament the course Mr. Garrison seems to be taking . . . ," he told Lewis Tappan — "I have no expectation that Garrison can be reduced to moderation, and I am not prepared to say that his departure from us may not be the best thing he could do for the cause of Emancipation." Lewis went to Boston and returned with no greater hope than Birney. Garrison and his friends obviously hoped to commit the entire abolitionist movement to an anticlerical war. The newspapers were already calling Garrison "the Prince of New England Infidelity," and he had opened the columns of the *Liberator* to freethinkers, agnostics, and assorted fanatics. Garrison probably intended, Isaac Knapp told Tappan, to turn the *Liberator* into a radical, antichurch, "no-government" publication, in which case Knapp promised to continue the paper himself as an abolitionist organ. Garrison's influence, Tappan believed, was on the wane; his battle with the clergy might be an opportunity to let him ride off in his own direction and out of the movement. Elizur Wright agreed that Garrison was fast becoming a liability to the national society, while Gamaliel Bailey, working on the Cincinnati *Philanthropist,* thought that "gross egotism" had "driven Garrison mad."

The fall meeting of the Massachusetts society revealed more anti-Garrison feeling than even Birney and Tappan had realized. Abolitionists resented Garrison's arrogance, said Daniel Wise; Garrison ran the society "as if he were . . . supreme judge of all abolitionists." His "overgrown self-conceit," Phelps complained, "had wrought him into the belief that his mighty self was abolition incarnate." Others had qualms about his battle with the clergy. Still others disapproved of "no-government" doctrines and of his editorial vocabulary. The split within the society, according to Birney, was threefold: a conservative, anti-Garrisonian group, mostly clergymen, who opposed his war with the ministry and his addiction to radical reforms; an evangelical group, led by Phelps, which opposed Garrison's espousal of non-abolitionist reforms but which supported him in his attacks on the orthodox clergy; and those loyal Garrisonians — May, Johnson, Foster, Burleigh, H. C. Wright, and others — who were "bent on war to the knife and knife to the hilt" against anyone who disagreed with Garrison.

The convention did not, as Birney and Tappan feared, break out in an open revolt. The *Liberator* had been running an annual deficit of more than a thousand dollars since 1833, and some of the society's members were unwilling to continue to finance it if it were to be simply an anticlerical propaganda sheet. Others believed that if it were to remain the society's semiofficial organ, it should reflect the society's rather than Garrison's views, which many did not wish to defend. Garrison, for once, was willing to make peace. He suggested that the society withdraw its support from the *Liberator*, leaving it an independent paper. The society quickly agreed. Accordingly the *Liberator* announced its independence, "through a desire to remove those scruples or doubts which may exist . . . even though they are confined to the breasts of a few individuals." This was a minor victory for the anti-Garrisonians, but their only one.

As soon as the *Liberator* cut loose from the Massachusetts society, Garrison announced a new editorial policy. The abolition of slavery, he wrote in his prospectus for 1838, would still be "the grand object of our labors, though not, perhaps, so exclusively as before"; the *Liberator* would also work for peace, for women's rights, and for the "universal emancipation of all humanity from all bondage to human government." A new department appeared in the paper, headed "Equal Rights," and another new column, "Non Resistance," appeared on page four. Since Garrison's health bothered him throughout the year, he left most of the editorial responsibility to Oliver Johnson, making only occasional calls at his offices and sending in his own editorials by mail. He spent much time at his home in Brookline, leaving it only for important meetings. He attended the American Antislavery Society's convention in New York in early 1838, moved on to Philadelphia for the American Antislavery Women's Convention, and returned to Boston in time for the May convention of the New England antislavery societies. At this last meeting Oliver Johnson introduced a "woman" resolution, naming all female delegates as voting members of the convention. Abby Kelley, a sharp-tongued Irishwoman from Boston, provided the fireworks in the debate, and the resolution passed. Fifteen delegates, including Phelps and Torrey of the Massachusetts group, asked to have their names expunged from the convention rolls in protest.

The presence in Boston of delegates from all New England was too good an opportunity for Garrison to miss.

Calling a meeting of "friends of peace," he proposed that a convention be held in September to discuss the organization of a new national peace society. Garrison was already a member of the American Peace Society, but he had long ago concluded it lacked aggressiveness. His correspondence with Noyes and his discussions with the Quaker Grimké sisters convinced him that simple pacifism was not enough. Christians must not only work actively for peace, Garrison explained; they must also refuse allegiance to any government not based on pacifistic principles. Since all governments maintained themselves ultimately by military force, he reasoned, the true pacifist could not in conscience recognize the validity of any government whatever — a position consistent with both pacifist and Noyesian "no-government" doctrines.

The Peace Convention attracted about two hundred delegates, more than half of them from Massachusetts. May, Wright, Quincy, Phillips, Abby Kelley, Amasa Walker, and Bronson Alcott attended with Garrison, and the *pro tem* officers of the convention were all Garrisonian abolitionists. After the usual speeches and resolutions, the meeting assigned Garrison the task of composing the customary Declaration of Sentiments.

Garrison's Declaration was, as he said, "radical in all things." It denied allegiance to any government, refused to recognize any state or national boundaries, and rejected distinctions of class, sex, or race made by society — for, he reminded the delegates, "Our country is the world, and our countrymen all mankind." He recommended the abolition of navies, armies, military laws, ranks, or titles, all monuments or holidays commemorating military victories, all military orders and trophies, all appropriations for armaments, and all laws of conscription. Society members, he believed, should not "resist the operation of laws except by meekly submitting to the penalty of disobedience" (a position for which Tolstoy later praised him). But they must also "voluntarily exclude themselves from every legislative and judicial body, and repudiate all human politics, worldly honors, and stations of authority."

Anarchy, however Christian it might be, was more than May, Quincy, and Phillips had bargained for. None of them signed the declaration, though the convention adopted it without much debate and launched on the formal organization of the New England Non-Resistance Society. The American Peace Society and the New York Peace Society, the most highly respected and influential antiwar organizations in the country, hurriedly repudiated the Garrisonian group.

Nonresistance, added to "no-government," women's rights, and anticlericalism, was too much for some members of the Massachusetts Antislavery Society to bear. Amos Phelps resigned his post as agent in protest, and Garrison's friends held worried consultations. To compound the trouble, the *Liberator* was in a bad way: creditors hounded Garrison, the recently married Knapp wanted a regular salary, and Garrison had overreached himself by promising to publish the new peace society's paper, the *Non Resistant*. There was real danger that the *Liberator* might fail. A committee of Jackson, Quincy, and William Bassett (later Loring and Samuel Philbrick were added) agreed to pay some of its debts and supervise its finances if Oliver Johnson remained as assistant editor to bring a little order to its publication. Knapp was satisfied to have a few columns of advertising space to sell for his own profit, and much to Garrison's relief the books nearly balanced.

As the Massachusetts society prepared for its annual meeting in January, 1839, there were strong signs that Garrison's authority was about to be challenged again. "Strong foes are without, insidious plotters are within the camp," Garrison told his friends. Phelps and Torrey, he believed, were busy consolidating opposition, while Henry B. Stanton from New York was in Massachusetts, covertly working against him. At a meeting of the Middlesex Society, Stanton appeared with a resolution that any person who had signed the Declaration of the Non-Resistant Society was automatically disqualified for membership in the American Antislavery Society. Although the resolution never went beyond the discussion stage, remarks passed that were highly critical of Garrison, and he heard of them. "Will you," he asked May, "throw out the signals to all loyal Garrisonians?" "The spirit which assails us," he warned *Liberator* readers, "is proscriptive and contemptible."

The Massachusetts society's meeting opened on January 23, 1839, Francis Jackson presiding. Phelps and Torrey lost no time in launching their attack. Garrison, they said, had muddled the abolition movement, alienated public opinion, and confused the main issue with capricious diversions. "This society," said Phelps, "is no longer an antislavery society, but in its principles and modes of action a women's rights, non-government, antislavery society." He and others did not want a society in which "they must take non-resistance, women's rights, perfectionism, etc., too." A new paper, said Torrey, was indispensable to the abolitionist cause in New England. The *Liberator* refused to prick abolition voters to their duty at the polls, published long disquisitions on "subjects injurious to the cause," and "lowered the standard of abolition." What was needed was a weekly organ devoted to political action, a paper from which matters extraneous to abolition were excluded, and one under the direct control of the society's executive board.

Garrison's friends, however, were there in force. He refused to retreat an inch, and Phillips and Loring eloquently defended his course. As a result Torrey's demand for a new paper never came to a vote. Stanton made the next move, presenting a resolution declaring that "every member of an antislavery society" who refused to vote was "guilty of gross inconsistency, and widely departs from the original and fundamental principles of the antislavery enterprise." His motion lost, almost unanimously. Phelps's attempt to exclude female members from the vote was ruled out of order by Jackson. Alanson St. Clair, a Phelps supporter, offered a resolution that "every abolitionist who could *conscientiously* do so" should go to the polls, but Garrison refused to accept the compromise and the meeting voted it down.

It was perfectly apparent, after three failures, that Garrison had the votes, and the "conspirators" admitted defeat. Since the Massachusetts society obviously would continue to follow Garrison wherever he proposed to go, Phelps and the dissidents withdrew to issue a call for a new antislavery society, free from Garrisonian influence. Stanton took charge, planned an organizational meeting, and prepared to found a new paper, the *Massachusetts Abolitionist,* to be edited by Phelps and a committee of twenty-seven. With the new *Abolitionist* and the *Liberator* to choose between, said Daniel Wise, antislavery men could at least "have the hairs served on one plate and the butter on another."

Garrison expressed no surprise at the break, and was uncommonly charitable at first to the rebels. More than anything else, he said, he was glad that his long-suspected enemies were "no longer secret, but have left the forests and swamps for an open field." So far as the *Liberator* was concerned, he denied any intention of using it as "a medium through which to promulgate . . . any peculiar theological sentiments," but he would most assuredly continue "to devote a small portion" of it to discussions of any reform he cared to espouse. Henry Stanton, thought Garrison, was at the root of the trouble. "His conduct has been reprehensible throughout," Garrison bitterly told George Benson, "and . . . his political hobby has wellnigh ruined him."

After the meeting Stanton sent a gloomy report to the executive committee in New York. The Garrisonians had won, chiefly with the help of the votes of the women from Boston and Lynn. Garrison and Wright, Stanton believed, were determined to "rule or ruin the antislavery cause." The abolitionist movement in Massachusetts, he concluded, was doomed "unless we can separate the American Antislavery Society from everything that does not belong to it." Elizur Wright, like Stanton, thought that the Massachusetts split threatened the existence of abolitionism in all New England. Garrison, wrote W. G. Burleigh, was "bent on making abolitionism a stalking-horse for no-governmentism, no-churchism, and every other insane whim." On Stanton's advice the executive committee informed the Massachusetts society that it was cancelling its financial agreements, and that the national society intended to send agents into Massachusetts to solicit contributions. Although Phillips and Henry Chapman went to

New York to protest, the committee refused to change its decision. In March, with repudiation by the national society staring it in the face, the Massachusetts society met again, this time with Lewis Tappan and James Birney from the New York office. Neither Tappan nor Birney could find any grounds for reconciliation so long as Garrison refused to listen to talk of compromise with the Phelps-Torrey-St. Clair "conspirators."

Garrison's own friends stood by him loyally. "William Lloyd Garrison is *an historical fact* in the annals of antislavery," a meeting of "The Friends of William Lloyd Garrison" resolved, "and every abolitionist . . . ought to sustain him." "Far from deeming the course of the *Liberator* faulty in respect to political action, we look upon the ground it has occupied," resolved another meeting, "as the only one on which any antislavery periodical can stand." The Phelps-Torrey rebels at their meetings passed resolutions as censorious as the Garrisonians' were complimentary, and the battle of resolutions blazed through the spring. "The spirit of the Massachusetts belligerents," reported Theodore Weld, "is absolutely ferocious," with every issue of the *Liberator* "filled with the vibrations of serpents' tongues." Garrison took to the road, flaying the secessionists in town after town in Massachusetts and counseling open rebellion against the New York Committee. Phelps, Torrey, and the anti-Garrisonians toured the state too. Both sides jockeyed for position, waiting for the American Antislavery Society's annual convention in early May.

At the national convention, the contest ended in a draw. On the first clash, over a resolution granting female delegates the right to speak and vote, the Garrisonians won, 180-140. The executive committee countered with the statement that this resolution did not commit the society to support "any controverted principle respecting the rights of women," and 116 anti-Garrison delegates signed a petition declaring the action unconstitutional.

The second clash, over the desirability of political action, led to a defeat for Garrison, but Whittier successfully introduced a compromise motion defining voting as "a high obligation — a duty," but not a requirement for abolitionists. Finally the election of officers showed that control of the society remained with the New York group, for Birney, Stanton, Leavitt, Weld, and the others were returned to office without significant opposition.

At the New England Antislavery Convention, which met a few days later in Boston, Garrison made short shrift of Phelps and Torrey. Phelps brought up the question of women's rights and the Garrisonians voted him down. Next they passed a resolution condemning the formation of any new antislavery society in Massachusetts, and then another, exhorting "true abolitionists" to abstain from politics. That was enough for the anti-Garrisonians. On the second day of the convention they left to form the Massachusetts Abolition Society and to get away from Garrison for once and all. "The sober, serious, prayerful, and religious abolitionists are mostly with us in the city," wrote Phelps, "and the weight of character with us in the country." The new society at once sent a request to the New York executive committee, asking that it be officially recognized as the state society representing Massachusetts, while Garrison followed it with a letter of protest. How the real balance of power lay in New England abolitionist circles neither Birney nor Stanton knew, so the New York committee took no decisive action and bided its time.

In July the National Convention of Abolitionists invited delegates from all local, state, and national societies to meet in Albany. The primary issue would be — and everyone knew it — the advisability of forming a political party on abolitionist principles. The American Antislavery Society's leaders (except Lewis Tappan) favored it; so did Alvan Stewart, Myron Holley, and the leaders of the powerful New York State Society. Though Garrison himself had once urged the formation of "a Christian party in politics" to agitate the slavery question, he had long since abandoned the idea. His "no-government" policies barred him from participation in any form of politics, for only moral force, in his opinion, could abolish slavery. Political action, with its implicit recognition of the existence of a civil government and of that government's power to regulate human affairs, was to Garrison fundamentally sinful.

The Albany convention proved a rather tame affair. Of the five hundred delegates, some sixty were Garrisonians. They were steam-rollered flat by the committee on arrangements, which ruled at the beginning that all "extraneous matters" must be excluded from the convention. Garrison, with no chance to discuss women's rights, "no-government," and political action, sat out the three-day meeting in disgust. No abolitionist, the meeting went on to resolve, should support a candidate who had not declared himself unequivocally for immediatism; every abolitionist must vote; all abolitionists should adopt that course of action politically best fitted to the area in which they lived. All the resolutions pointed to the impending creation of a third party for the presidential elections of 1840, and after the convention closed the political-actionists moved rapidly. In September the Monroe County Society in New York went on record in favor of a national abolitionist party ticket. In October the American Antislavery Society called a political meeting in Cleveland. In November, the New York State society met in convention and nominated Birney (who declined) for president on an abolition ticket, also issuing a call for a national convention to prepare for a national campaign. Garrison, who would have none of the affair, called these maneuverings "impure, divisive, and diversionary" and advised his followers to avoid them.

Garrison had in mind another and bigger objective — the capture of the American Antislavery Society itself. The national society existed on the edge of financial ruin, which even the Tappans' seemingly inexhaustible fortune was unable to avert. The difficulty lay in its agreement to solicit no contributions from areas controlled by state societies, which, as they grew larger and more powerful, gradually cut off its income. Since the Ohio, New York State, and Massachusetts societies covered the most populous areas of the North, by 1839 the national society could call very little territory its own. The state societies, which were supposed to contribute funds directly to the parent society's treasury, gave reluctant pledges to do so and often failed to honor them. In Massachusetts alone, the annual sums collected by the national society dropped from ten thousand to five hundred dollars in a few years. The New York executive committee asked permission to send its agents into Massachusetts to solicit direct contributions, but Garrison refused. In 1839 the American Antislavery Society notified its field agents that they must collect their own salaries, and sent Birney on an emergency tour to talk directly to the state society leaders. He found them critical of the national office, jealous of their independence, and extremely slow in meeting pledges of financial support.

Things in the New York office went from bad to worse. Salaries were nearly a year in arrears, neither agents nor printers had been paid, and the books showed $6590 in outstanding debts. In January, 1840, the executive committee called an emergency meeting, discussed the financial situation, and appointed Birney, Lewis Tappan, and James Gibbons as a subcommittee to decide the society's fate. The best that the American Antislavery Society could do, the three concluded, was to pay as many of its debts as possible and dissolve. Some creditors were paid off in books from stock, officeworkers were released, and preparations made for the transfer of the *Emancipator* to the New York City society. The state societies promised to help liquidate the indebtedness, and everyone assumed that at the next annual convention the national society would be voted out of existence.

Garrison had no intention of allowing this to happen. A national organization was too valuable to lose. He wanted the American Antislavery Society to continue as a nonresistant, antipolitical, no-government, abolition society, and he wanted to control it. There was another problem to settle first, however — the meeting called in April at Albany to launch a political party. The Massachusetts society, the Lynn society, and the Boston society dutifully passed resolutions against political action, while Garrison wrote a pamphlet exhorting abolitionists to oppose "that small but talented body of restless and ambitious men" who hoped to lead them into partisan politics. Abolition, he wrote, "is a moral contest"; a political party could not be both

moral and successful; politics emphasized men and not issues; a political party recognized the validity of law and
government, thus implying its willingness to abide by them.
Reform and politics were simply not miscible.

The convention brushed Garrison and his group aside.
Of its 121 delegates, 104 came from New York State, the
stronghold of political action, and the meeting proceeded
to create the Liberty Party, nominate Birney again for
President, and prepare for a campaign. Garrison, dismiss-
ing the affair as "folly, presumption, and almost unequaled
infatuation," went back to Boston to wait for the American
Antislavery Society's convention — but without Samuel Sewall, who joined the Liberty Party after nine years at Garrison's side.

The Garrisonian group in New England viewed the argument over political action as the sole cause of the division in abolitionist ranks. Stanton, Birney, and Leavitt in
New York City, Holley, Smith, and Stewart of the New
York State Society, Phelps, Torrey, and Orange Scott in
Massachusetts were all, according to Henry Wright, "determined to organize a great political party, to regenerate
the government." At the May meeting, the Garrisonians
predicted, the political-actionists would "make a desperate
push . . . to convert the Parent Society into a political
party." There was some truth in Garrison's charge that the
politicians were at work to commit the abolitionist movement to partisan politics. There was, however, another
reason for the split — a growing belief that Garrison's principles and tactics were divisive, diversionary, and irresponsible; that nonresistance, "no-government," women's
rights, and anticlericalism had no place within a reform
movement wholly concerned with a specific reform. "The

true question," Leavitt wrote in the *Emancipator,* was whether or not abolitionism was to be "controlled *at pleasure* . . . by a single auxiliary society . . . representing a section of abolitionists of a single state." Abolition and non-resistance or abolition and "no-government," in Goodell's opinion, "can no more walk together than abolition and colonization." Antislavery could brook no popes, said Goodell, nor should it scatter its force to the four winds. The question of who ruled the movement would obviously be settled at the American Antislavery Society's annual New York convention.

"If you would preserve it from the spirit which is seeking to dash it to fragments," read the Massachusetts society's appeal for delegates to the national convention of 1840, "then you will throng to the anniversary of the parent society on the 12th of May next." Garrison sent Henry Wright to Philadelphia to sound the alarm, and Lewis Tappan in New York wrote Weld that "Garrison has three or four men here, beating the bushes." "I loathe the spirit that comes from the East," Lewis wrote despondently. "Our organization is a stench in the nostrils of the nation and the approaching meeting will increase it." John Collins, an Andover graduate who had joined Garrison a year earlier, and the faithful Oliver Johnson were placed in charge of collecting New England delegates. Collins chartered a steamboat, tied it up at Providence, and on May 11 the delegates began to pour into Boston. The 1839 resolution of the society, recognizing women as delegates, worked to Garrison's advantage. The ladies from Lynn and Boston swarmed into town, solidly pro-Garrison, and when the *Rhode Island* sailed for New York it carried 450 delegates, 410 from Massachusetts and the majority of them women.

"It was our antislavery boatload," Garrison said later, "that saved our society from falling into the hands of the new organizers, or rather disorganizers."

The convention assembled on May 12, 1840, at the Fourth Free Church of New York. More than a thousand delegates appeared, the largest attendance in the society's history. Arthur Tappan, the society's president, turned the chair over to vice-president Francis Jackson from Boston, and the Garrisonians went into action. Jackson appointed the temporary committees, dividing personnel fairly evenly between known Garrisonians and anti-Garrisonians, but he deliberately placed Abby Kelley on the business committee. The "woman question" started and finished the battle. "To put a woman on the committee with men," Lewis Tappan said, "is contrary to the Constitution of the Society; it is throwing a firebrand into the antislavery ranks; it is contrary to the usages of civilized society." But the anti-Garrisonians simply did not have the votes. The convention approved Jackson's appointments 560-450, and Abby stayed on the committee. Amos Phelps and C. W. Denison immediately resigned, and, speaking from the floor, asked all those who had voted against Abby's confirmation to withdraw from the convention for the purpose of forming a new society. Arthur Tappan followed them out, surrendering the presidency of the society he had done so much to create, and the entire executive committee (except Quaker James Gibbons) went with him. "I hope," said Tappan sadly, "that God may override the machinations of the disorganizers against us, and save us from the disgrace I apprehend."

The convention continued with the Garrisonians in full control. Lucretia Mott, Lydia Child, and Maria Chapman went on the executive committee by a virtually unanimous vote. A resolution condemning political action aroused some debate, but it passed in watered-down form. Another resolution protested the transfer of the *Emancipator* to the city society — "plain swindling," said Wendell Phillips — and appointed a committee to negotiate for its return. Next, the meeting resolved to send delegates to the World Antislavery Convention in London; and as an afterthought, almost impudently, it approved a typically Garrisonian resolution to the effect that the organized churches were "foes of freedom, humanity, and pure religion," giving "undisguised sanction and support to slavery." "We have made clean work of everything," Garrison wrote joyfully to his wife, "adopted the most thoroughgoing resolutions, and taken the strongest ground, with crashing unanimity." The American Antislavery Society belonged to William Lloyd Garrison, lock, stock, and barrel.

Fresh from his triumph in New York, Garrison embarked for the World Antislavery Convention in London in high spirits. The London society in its original invitation had indicated that "gentlemen only were expected to attend," since the British were well aware of the "unhappy dissention" over women's rights that plagued the Americans. Though the Londoners wrote directly to Francis Jackson that "the admission of women is not contemplated," Garrison advised the Massachusetts Society to include a number of them in its delegation, while the Pennsylvania Society sent the redoubtable Lucretia Mott. With Garrison busy in New York, Wendell Phillips and the delegates from Massachusetts went ahead to London. Birney and Stanton from the New York group and Gerrit Smith from the New York State society also left early. Garrison, N. P.

Rogers, William Adams, and Charles Remond arrived after the convention had been in session for five days, and after Phillips had already started the fight over women's rights.

The day before Garrison's arrival, Phillips moved the appointment of a committee of five to prepare a list of convention delegates, "to include the names of *all* persons bearing credentials from any antislavery society" — the same strategy over the "woman question" employed at New York. The British were not easily bluffed, and instead the convention adopted a substitute motion barring women from the list. Garrison, arriving in time to learn of the defeat, refused to present his credentials or to take his seat as a delegate. Glowering in the gallery, surrounded by rejected females, he waited out the convention, causing in Birney's opinion "a good deal of merriment" among the British.

Despite his dramatic secession, the convention went on with its business, with Birney and Gerrit Smith representing the American societies. On July 9 Garrison spoke at Freemason's Hall — a rambling, ineffective speech, said Elizabeth Cady Stanton disappointedly — and traveled on to Scotland and Ireland to attend a few antislavery meetings. On August 4 he left for home.

Garrison arrived in Boston in time to attend the closing sessions of the Christian Union Convention in Groton, and to prepare for the New England Non-Resistance Convention, slated for Boston's Chardon Street Chapel a week later. In November he appeared at the Chardon Street Convention of Universal Reformers, the most famous reform meeting of the decade, at which nonresistants, abolitionists, transcendentalists, Quakers, women's rights advocates, temperance workers, and assorted reformers all had their say — "a great deal of confusion, eccentricity and freak appeared," said Emerson, who did not go, "as well as of zeal and enthusiasm."

During Garrison's absence in London the American Antislavery Society moved its offices to Nassau Street near Beekman in New York City, placing Isaac Hopper, the old Quaker, in charge. A new executive committee went in, solidly Garrisonian, and authorized a new paper to replace the lost *Emancipator:* the *National Antislavery Standard.* The committee gave the editorship to Lydia Maria Child and her husband David, followed by Sydney Gay, and eventually Oliver Johnson. The national society next sent out a call for money, but the state and local societies failed to respond; accordingly it dispatched James Collins to England to solicit British funds. Collins had only mild success. Charles Stuart and John Scoble spread the word that the American Antislavery Society under Garrisonian leadership was simply "a pernicious party" run by "Infidel Abolitionists" whose doctrines alienated respectable support everywhere in America. Although Garrison complained that his enemies abroad "spared no pains and let slip no opportunity to make me odious," Collins did succeed in gathering one thousand dollars, just in time to save the *Standard* from collapse.

Garrison's capture of the American Antislavery Society destroyed it as an effective abolitionist instrument. Its main strength after 1840 lay in Massachusetts, primarily in Boston and Lynn. The smaller New Hampshire and Pennsylvania state societies cleaved to the Garrisonian standard. The Western Antislavery Society, founded in 1845, followed his lead, but neither the Western society nor its organ, the *Antislavery Bugle,* carried much weight. Financial troubles constantly plagued the national society, and after a few years it moved its offices to Boston, leaving the *Standard* behind in New York to snipe at the opposition as "traitors and apostates." The society continued to hold its yearly meetings in New York, but it published no annual reports, and for the remainder of its existence did little more than serve as a sounding board for Garrisonian doctrine. Its executive committee sent out a few agents, but its membership drives were uniformly disappointing. At its maximum, the national society after 1840 counted no more than six hundred members, probably less than half of them active. Nevertheless, the society continued to function as a propaganda organization within the abolitionist movement, making converts and publicizing the moral aspects of the controversy. Garrison and Phillips were, whatever their antipathy to political action, redoubtable recruiting officers. Garrison's fervency and Phillips's golden tongue made hundreds of abolitionists, but could not keep them pure. They "run right into the Liberty Party," Phillips wrote sadly, "and become almost wholly hostile to us."

After the 1840 schism the anti-Garrison dissenters founded the American and Foreign Antislavery Society, hoping to reorganize the abolitionist movement about a new nucleus. But the powerful state societies and auxiliaries refused to join, having no desire to vest centralized control of the movement in any Eastern-based organization. National societies, thought Gerrit Smith, had lost their usefulness; they simply continued the old quarrels and aggravated division. Birney, Stanton, and Leavitt all retired, admitting defeat. Lewis Tappan alone kept the new society in existence. He kept in touch with the British, gathered funds for the *Amistad* captives, and helped to found the *National Era*. But the American and Foreign Antislavery Society, like Garrison's organization, exerted comparatively little influence in abolitionist affairs and finally died in 1853.

The truth of the matter was that after 1840 abolition was no longer a moral but a political issue. The split in the American Antislavery Society, at bottom, was the result of disagreement over political action, as Garrison correctly assumed — though his own addiction to women's rights, religious unorthodoxy, "no-government," and nonresistance, as well as his imperious self-righteousness, were factors that helped to force the division. Western abolitionists, already committed to political action, paid little attention to factional strife in the East, nor could the New Yorkers, deep in Liberty Party politics, find any good use for Garrison's or Tappan's organizations. More and more abolitionists believed after 1840 that success lay in politics, in the Liberty Party, in the Free-Soil Party, and eventually in the Republican Party. Beginning in 1837 Weld and Leavitt maintained an abolitionist lobby in Washington, and with the appearance in Congress of such men as J. Q. Adams, Morris, Slade, Giddings, Mattocks, and Andrews, the center of abolitionism gradually moved to the national capital. By 1856 abolitionism was the great political issue facing the nation — a question with moral implications, but one that could be answered only in political terms. All that was left of the old moral crusade against slavery was its fervor, which passed undiminished into politics. The vote of the old abolitionist territories, state by state, made Lincoln president.

V

No Union with Slaveholders

In 1841, William Lloyd Garrison held undisputed leadership of the "true" or "moral" wing of the abolition movement and complete control of the leading national antislavery society. Birney, Stanton, Leavitt, and the rest might go their way into partisan politics; Garrison hewed to the line of pure and original abolitionism. They, not he, had departed from the faith. The great schism of 1840 cleared the atmosphere and eventually had a salutary effect on the total organization of the movement. There were some private bitternesses, but less public display of antagonism than might have been expected. Each wing of abolitionism considered the other sincere, though misguided and ineffective, and at times there were grounds for wavering cooperation.

Garrison held New England in the palm of his hand. Henry Stanton thought that his "ultraism" was losing ground in Massachusetts, but that was wishful thinking. Garrison's support may have been regional, but his reputation was national. Despite his unpredictable enthusiasm for minor reforms and his editorial intransigeance, he was still an effective speaker and a tireless crusader. "I am covered all over with applications to lecture," Garrison wrote in

1841, and for the next three years he found eager audiences from Maine to Ohio for talks on abolition, women's rights, peace, the Sabbath, or for that matter any topic he cared to discuss. With him on tour he often took Fred Douglass, an escaped slave whom the Massachusetts society hired as agent — an imposing figure of a man, a persuasive speaker, and living proof of what freedom meant to the Negro.

The *Non Resistant* died in 1842 from lack of funds, but the *Liberator* struggled along despite an unhappy interlude with Isaac Knapp. After severing connections with the paper for a cash payment of seventy-five dollars, Knapp mulled over the arrangement and decided he had been badly treated. Before his printing contract expired in January, 1842, he concluded that he had been forced out by the "treachery and duplicity" of the Boston clique. The *Liberator*, he maintained, was no longer a "free discussion paper," but a Garrisonian sheet pure and simple. *Knapp's Liberator*, he announced, would return to the old antislavery policy, and subscribers who disliked Garrisonism would find it more to their taste. Not many, evidently, disliked Garrison's paper, for *Knapp's Liberator* lasted exactly one issue.

The *Liberator* itself continued to give space to discussions of dueling, tobacco-using, cockfighting, cruelty to animals, diet, fashions, women's rights, nonresistance, "nogovernment," or any other reform Garrison happened to find interesting. The death in 1842 of his brother James, whom he had rescued from the Navy as a hopeless alcoholic three years earlier, lent an especial urgency to his temperance crusade. His own weak health (he suffered from exhaustion and headaches) made Garrison an easy mark for patent medicines, spiritualistic seances, and special diets, to which he often gave large amounts of free advertising. His friends occasionally expostulated with him over the *Liberator's* instability. A reader never knew what new cause he might find suddenly spread out in its pages. Quincy, who often served as editor in Garrison's absence, complained that the paper had no editorial policies at all; it was a "higgledy-piggledy" sheet, hastily made up, carelessly written, mirroring the mood of the moment. Quincy was quite right, and the reason was easy to see. The *Liberator* was Garrison's journalistic alter ego, reflecting (even when Johnson or Quincy took over) his own hastily made-up, unpredictable mind.

"We do not know of a single antislavery paper that sustains itself," Joseph Lovejoy wrote in 1841. Garrison's *Liberator* was no exception. Its subscription list was never more than twenty-five hundred, usually less. It made monthly appeals for "FUNDS, FUNDS, FUNDS!" It held out bonuses for subscriptions, begged for donations, and even offered to sell a portrait of Garrison, "engraved on shell," for a dollar. At that, it was more solvent than most of the other antislavery publications. The *National Antislavery Standard*, always teetering on the brink of failure, never found an editor (until Oliver Johnson) who could satisfy Garrison. The *Pennsylvania Freeman* died in 1841; revived by Burleigh and McKim, both ardent Garrisonians, it did somewhat better but never well. The *Herald of Freedom* in New Hampshire, edited by Nathaniel Rogers, followed the *Liberator's* line until Rogers and Garrison had a falling out; Parker Pillsbury, who took it over after Rogers's death, never made it a success. The *Antislavery Bugle* in Ohio, edited first by Oliver Johnson, later by the Quakers Benjamin and Elizabeth Jones, and still later by Marius Robinson, had neither wide circulation nor influence.

Other antislavery publications took up the cause of political action after 1840 and turned into party organs. Lovejoy in 1842 listed nineteen newspapers which favored the Liberty Party and sixteen which "were not hostile." The *Emancipator,* owned by Lewis Tappan's American and Foreign Antislavery Society and edited by Joshua Leavitt, moved to Boston in 1841, became a Liberty Party journal, merged with several other Liberty papers, and finally died in 1850. Goodell's *Friend of Man,* in Utica, New York, went sled-length into politics. Myron Holley, an avowed political abolitionist, founded and edited the Rochester *Freeman;* Charles Torrey's Syracuse *Tocsin of Liberty* (renamed the *Patriot*) was another Liberty paper, and so was the Cincinnati *Philanthropist,* edited after Birney's departure by Gamaliel Bailey. Joseph Lovejoy edited the Hallowell, Maine, *Advocate of Freedom,* renamed it the *Liberty Standard* in 1841 and the *Free-Soil Republican* in 1848, thus moving with the times.

The founding of the *National Era* by the American and Foreign Antislavery Society in 1847 began another kind of reform journalism. Gamaliel Bailey made it into a sharp, well-edited, thoroughly readable newspaper, one of the best of the period and certainly the best of the antislavery publications. Garrison's *Liberator,* by contrast, remained until its last issue the same highly personalized, belligerent, and hastily edited journal it had been since 1831. "Those who like ebullitions of wrath and columns of abuse may like his paper," Gerrit Smith said of Garrison. Out of all the hundreds of thousands of supporters claimed by the abolitionists after 1840, fewer than three thousand evidently did.

Garrison changed very little during the 1840's and '50's, and neither did the *Liberator*. He continued his war on clergymen — "the deadliest enemies of marriage, of the Bible, the weekly Sabbath, the *Christian* church and ministry, and of revivals of religion." Ministers, according to the *Liberator*, were "a brotherhood of thieves" (a phrase picked up in 1844 by Stephen Foster for the title of his violently anticlerical book) and "the haughty, corrupt, implacable, and pious foes of the anti-slavery movement." At every annual convention of the Massachusetts society after 1840, Garrison or his friends introduced resolutions condemning the clergy and the churches, and they always passed. "Steeped in blood and pollution as the American Church is," the society voted in a typical instance, "it becomes us to turn from it with loathing and abhorrence."

Henry C. Wright, Stephen S. Foster, Parker Pillsbury, and Abby Kelley (who after her marriage to Foster traveled with him) took anticlericalism on tour. In Wright's opinion, the churches preached "a religion that apologizes for concubinage, polygamy, heathenism — a religion that murders and steals," and he filled a column of the *Liberator* nearly every week with long arguments in support of his accusations. Foster and Pillsbury, who called themselves "Antislavery Apostles," were even more abusive. The Methodist Church, Foster said, was "a conclave of incarnate fiends"; the Presbyterians and Congregationalists "stole babes"; the Southern Baptists "sold GIRLS for wine for their communion tables"; Unitarians, Episcopalians, and Quakers were all "man-stealers." Quincy, May, and

Phillips occasionally objected to this unapostolic language, but Garrison consistently defended the "apostles."

During the 1840's Garrison also kept up an energetic campaign against the observance of the Sabbath. "I stand upon the Bible," he wrote, "and the Bible alone, in regard to my views of the Sabbath." In 1848 he proposed to call an Anti-Sabbath Convention "to rid the land of the spirit of religious bigotry and ecclesiastical tyranny." Phillips and May refused to have anything to do with it, while Parker and Quincy signed the announcement with the understanding that they would not attend. The convention met in early 1848, accomplishing nothing beyond long resolutions and the loss of Garrison's coat to a thief. Wright's articles on the meeting, published in the *Liberator*, aroused a great deal of comment, particularly his announcement that "the Bible was a self-evident falsehood." The subsequent protests seemed to Garrison to warrant calling a Bible Convention. The convention never met, but the call, Garrison calculated, cost him five hundred subscriptions to the *Liberator*. Quincy, after long talks with Garrison about religious faith, thought that Garrison was dangerously close to free thought. He read Theodore Parker's liberal Unitarian tracts avidly and held interminable discussions with Parker; references to Tom Paine and analyses of eighteenth-century deism appeared in the *Liberator* week after week.

Garrison's third trip to England came about chiefly because of his war with the clergy. The Free Church of Scotland, which seceded from the Established Scottish Church in 1843, made a drive for funds in the United States and received sizable sums from Southern Presbyterian churches. The Glasgow Emancipation Society, however, questioned the propriety of accepting money from "churches of slaveholders" and began a "Send Back the Money" campaign. Henry C. Wright (then in England) and George Thompson both rushed to Glasgow to give aid, and Thompson suggested that Garrison be invited to join them. Garrison's health was not strong, but the idea attracted him. Leaving the *Liberator* to Quincy, Phillips, and Maria Chapman, he sailed in July with Fred Douglass, Charles Remond, and James Buffum, "to protest against the foul deed of the Free Church of Scotland in putting in its treasury the price of blood."

Garrison and his friends stopped first in London to spend a few days at the World Temperance Convention, then in session. Lyman Beecher and other New Englanders, who were also there, allowed the Garrisonians precious little opportunity to express themselves, but Garrison had only mild interest in the convention anyway. He was much more concerned with persuading British abolitionists to form a new Antislavery League, distinct from the anti-Garrison British and Foreign Antislavery Society, and one with which his own national society might work. The old British society, he explained, was too tainted by its association with Tappan's American group to be of much help to him. The league was organized on August 10, 1846, at the Crown and Anchor Tavern, but influential British abolitionists avoided it. Nevertheless the new league held a public meeting the next week, before what Garrison called "an intelligent, respectable, and enthusiastic audience," though an admittedly small one. The Evangelical Alliance, composed chiefly of Methodists and Free Church

Presbyterians, met a week later and gave the league an issue by adopting a watered-down antislavery resolution.
Garrison and Thompson attended the league's protest
meeting and helped to pass a resolution censuring the alliance.

Garrison and Douglass spent nearly three months lectur-
ing in England and Scotland. The Free Church never did
send back the money, yet it was in other respects a successful tour. The impression left by the earnest white man
and the dignified black one was a lasting one, but, as the
Bristol *Mercury* remarked, Mr. Garrison would have
gained more support had he not used language "often re-
pulsive to English tastes."

Rebellious feelings about theological orthodoxy made
Garrison and other abolitionists impatient with social conformity and interested them in the numerous experi-
ments in communal living that flourished during the
decade. George Ripley, Emerson's friend, began a tran-
scendental-Fourieristic community at Brook Farm, hoping
to build "a New State and a New Church"; Adin Ballou,
who helped Garrison found the Non-Resistant Society,
founded a Christian-Communal Society at Hopedale. William Chace of the Massachusetts Antislavery Society decided it was a crime to earn a living except by gardening,
and established a one-man agricultural community of his
own. "Not a reading man but has the draft of a new community in his waistcoat pocket," Emerson noted in his
journals, and Garrison was attracted to all of them. Quincy,
May, and Phillips, who considered both anti-Sabbatarian-
ism and utopian communism dangerous diversions, argued
with him; Burleigh, Wright, Foster, Pillsbury, Maria

Chapman, and Francis Jackson encouraged him. When Garrison's favorite brother-in-law George Benson planned a community of his own in Northampton, Garrison almost joined it. In 1843 he moved to Benson's colony to live, but he could never bring himself to take out full membership. As his record showed, he was simply not an "association-ist." Organizations strait-jacketed him. Protest was better than conformity, even if the conformity was self-imposed.

By the mid-1840's, with nearly all Protestant sects in New England against him (except the Freewill Baptists) Garrison proceeded to embroil himself with the Catholics. General Catholic policy had been to avoid the slavery controversy on the ground that the institution was not in-herently incompatible with religion. The *Liberator* with-held comment until 1849, when Father Theobald Mat-thew, the Irish temperance lecturer, came to the United States. Father Matthew was a huge success. After admin-istering the pledge to 20,000 in New York and Brooklyn, he arrived in Boston. Garrison invited him to speak to the Massachusetts Antislavery Society, but Father Matthew, in some embarrassment, declined with the comment that he was interested in only one reform at a time, and that he knew of no clearly defined Biblical injunction against slavery. The *Liberator* immediately took him to task, ad-dressed a number of open letters to him, and censured him for his "neutrality" on a question of sin. The Boston Irish did not like it. The *New England Catholic Reporter,* no doubt reflecting the majority opinion of the Catholic press, called Garrison "a hoary hypocrite who . . . should be immediately transported to Ethiopia, there to dwell in all love and harmony with the wild negroes."

But Garrison's war with the Church was mild by comparison with his campaign against the Union and the Constitution. The constitutional status of slavery bothered the abolitionists, and until the question was settled by secession they could find no real basis for agreement among themselves. The South maintained from the outset that the Constitution recognized slavery on a national basis; interference with the system was therefore a violation of Southern rights. Many Northerners agreed. To this, one group of abolitionists replied that the Constitution was in reality an antislavery document — slavery was unconstitutional, illegal, and immediately to be abolished. Goodell, Lysander Spooner, and others argued in great detail that the Declaration of Independence abolished slavery by implication, and that the Constitution did not re-establish it; the system as it existed, therefore, clearly violated both. Another group of abolitionists believed the Constitution was neutral on the slavery issue, and that its abolition was not really a constitutional question; May, Birney, and Cassius Clay of Kentucky inclined to this view. Others believed that the framers of the Constitution had intended to outlaw slavery after 1808 but had left the matter for the action of later generations. Still others thought slavery violated the spirit though perhaps not the letter of the Constitution.

Garrison was neither equipped to deal with legal subtleties nor inclined to do so. The Constitution, he declared, both legalized and protected slavery — it was "a self-evident truth" that the American people were "morally incapable, through prejudice, hatred, and oppression," of framing a truly antislavery document. By recognizing slavery the Constitution violated human rights and Christian principles. Therefore the Constitution could not be regarded as law, nor should any union of states founded upon it be considered binding. On grounds of "abstract morality — of obedience to higher law," Garrison flatly refused to recognize the Constitution at all. "Friends of liberty and humanity," he wrote, "must immediately withdraw from the compact of bloody and deceitful men, to cease striking hands with adulterers."

Garrison's view placed him further than ever from the political-action abolitionists. If the Constitution was a neutral, or an antislavery document, the proper method of abolishing the system was by political means, as the Liberty Party and later the Radical Abolitionists agreed. If, however, the Constitution was a proslavery document, it must be bypassed or violated, and the Union founded on it destroyed. A "higher law" than man-made constitutions must "harmonize with the law of God or be set at naught by upright men," in the words of William Hosmer, the chief interpreter of the supra-legal school of Garrisonian abolitionists.

Garrison's uncompromising stand on the constitutional issue led his followers straight toward disunion. He developed his ideas gradually. As early as 1832 he asserted in the Liberator that "to continue the present compact" between the slave and free states was "in the highest degree criminal," and in 1833 he termed the Constitution "a most bloody and Heaven-daring arrangement . . . according to the law of God, null and void from the beginning." By 1842 he was disunionist in earnest. "We affirm," he wrote in that year, "that the Union is not of heaven. It is founded in unrighteousness and cemented in blood. . . . Slavery is a combination of Death and Hell, and with it the North have made a covenant and are at agreement."

At the January, 1842, meeting of the Massachusetts Antislavery Society, Garrison presented for the first time a resolution dealing with the disunion issue, but he did not force it to a vote. Because of ill health he did not attend the annual meeting of the American Antislavery Society in May, but Wright, Quincy, Phillips, and Abby Kelley all offered disunionist resolutions, finally accepting a compromise motion that the Constitution "should be so altered as to relieve the Federal government of responsibility for protecting slavery." At the New England Antislavery Convention a few days later, Quincy and Garrison renewed the discussion, while the *Liberator* broke out a new slogan at its masthead: "A Repeal of the Union between Northern Liberty and Southern Slavery is Essential to the Abolition of the One and the Preservation of the Other." Through 1842 Garrison appealed editorially week after week for a peaceful separation of North and South.

At the spring meeting of the Massachusetts society in 1843 Garrison believed it time to put the matter to a vote, offering a resolution that "the compact that exists between North and South is 'a covenant with death and an agreement with Hell' — involving both parties in atrocious criminality — and should be immediately annulled." It passed by a large majority, and the *Liberator* reworded its slogan — "No UNION WITH SLAVEHOLDERS!" — and kept the motto at its masthead until 1861. The political-action abolitionists quickly cleared their skirts of Garrisonian sentiments. Garrison's stand, they explained, was Garrison's alone. The Liberty Party convention at Syracuse formally condemned disunionism, and when Garrison chose to tour New York State in the summer of 1843, the Liberty abolitionists gave him an extremely cool reception.

The next step was to put the national American Antislavery Society on record in favor of disunion. At the annual convention of 1844 Garrison had a resolution ready, but Loring, Buffum, Thomas Earle, Burleigh, and Joseph McKim argued against it strenuously. Phillips carried the brunt of the disunion argument, neatly tying anticlericalism, abolition, and disunion into one package by declaring that only "through a dissolution of the Union and the overthrow of the organizations called Christian churches" could slavery be abolished. After three days of warm debate, the disunionists won. Henceforth the society and any of its members were "absolved from all religious and political allegiance with the organized church and the government of the United States."

The victory was not without its casualties. David Lee Child resigned his editorship of the *Standard* in protest, to be replaced by the more tractable Sydney Gay; and Ellis Gray Loring, his lawyer's soul outraged, resigned from the society. The New England Antislavery Convention, meeting a few days later, dutifully passed a similar disunion resolution by the overwhelming majority of 250 to 24. Through the year the other Garrisonian societies fell into line — the Western New York society, the Eastern Pennsylvania society, the new Ohio American Antislavery Society (soon renamed the Western), and scattered local societies in New England.

By 1846 the Garrisonian abolitionists presented a solidly disunionist front. The unhappy political-action aboli-

tionists, despite their loud denials, found themselves tarred
with the same brush. "Those who support the American
Antislavery Society and its agents support the worst enemies of the Liberty Party," warned the *Liberty Press,*
and Whig newspapers joyfully seized on the disunion issue
as election-time ammunition. "It is now almost universally
admitted," crowed the Cincinnati *Post,* "that the abolitionists are traitors, wicked hypocritical villains, *as a
body.*" That the American Antislavery Society represented
only Garrison made no difference; Birney ruefully admitted that it was virtually impossible to disassociate himself
and the Liberty Party from it.

But events had a way of swinging to Garrison's support.
The Mexican War, highly unpopular in New England, re-
cruited a number of allies for him. Many in Boston and its
environs regarded the war, as did Lowell's Yankee com-
mentator, "Hosea Biglow," as nothing more than an attempt "to lug new slave states in" so that the South might
have "bigger pens to cram." Lowell's Hosea spoke for
more than the abolitionists when he wrote, apropos of the
war and disunion:

> Ef I'd *my* way I hed ruther
>   We should go to work and part,
> They take one way, we take t'other,
>   Guess it wouldn't break my heart.
> Men had ough' to put asunder
>   Them that God has no ways jined,
> An' I shouldn't greatly wonder
>   Ef there's thousands o' my mind.

After the conflict, and with the onset of the postwar
agreement over the question of extending slavery into the

newly acquired Western territory, a good many "respectable" men agreed with Garrison and Hosea about a peaceful separation of slave and free states.

Exactly what Garrison meant by "No Union with Slaveholders!" was never quite clear. His stand on disunion was another instance of his method of attack — state the argument in general moral terms that few could conscientiously deny, and then let someone else worry over the practical implications. The Union, Garrison said, since it existed under a proslavery Constitution, was "infamous and accursed." No man who opposed slavery could rightfully take an oath to support that Constitution, obey any law passed under its terms, vote for any political candidate who was pledged to support it, or recognize any union of states based on it. The consequences of this Garrison never bothered to discuss at length. Should a new antislavery Constitution be drafted for the free states after the separation was accomplished? What disposition should be made of the District of Columbia, of the Federal territories, or of Congress itself? What of discriminatory "black laws" in the Northern free states? What might be the status of free Negroes in the South after disunion? None of these were really pertinent questions, in Garrison's opinion; the only issue was "the abrogation of the present pro-slavery constitution and the dissolution of the existing slaveholding union." "I am," he told George Benson, "simply an American Repealer."

Garrison's stubborn anticonstitutionalism stripped more of the faithful away from his side. During their tour of England, he and Douglass discussed political action and disunionism thoroughly, with Douglass holding out for the creation of an abolitionist party. After their return Douglass bought his freedom with funds partially raised in England, and the two set out for a similar tour of the West. Rowdiness and disorder followed them, since some communities resented a black man's presence on the platform, while Garrison, ill with a fever, finally canceled his engagements and stayed in Cleveland until he recovered. Douglass wanted to found a newspaper devoted to political action, and coolness developed between the two men. Shortly after leaving Garrison in Cleveland, Douglass started the *North Star* in Rochester, New York, backed by the politically minded New York State abolitionists. At almost the same time Tappan's American and Foreign Antislavery Society announced the appearance of the *National Era*, another political-action paper. Garrison strongly disapproved of both and said so.

The founding of Douglass's *North Star* and Bailey's *National Era* simply underscored a matter of plain fact — the division between Garrisonians and non-Garrisonians over political action was irreparably wide. "All hope of reunion is out of the question," Lewis Tappan wrote. "The warfare between the old organization — which is in possession of the name of the American Antislavery Society — and the New Organization, including the Liberty Party — is unrelenting." This intramural bickering troubled many abolitionist leaders, who offered olive branches to Garrison every year. "In the name of the poor slave," Goodell begged him, "let us cease quarreling, or seeming to quarrel, on the question of which of us has got hold of the best weapons of accomplishment. . . ." Garrison never responded, and the *Liberator* continued to berate "the cant and duplicity" of those "political hypocrites" who claimed to be both abolitionists and politicians. Joshua Leavitt's editorials in the *Emancipator and Free American,* a paper Garrison particularly disliked, he usually reprinted in his "Refuge of Oppression" column, along with proslavery editorials from Southern journals. Bailey, the able editor of the *Era,* he simply dismissed as a man "well supplied with self-esteem . . . with a fair share of talent, but with a lack of moral abhorrence of wrong-doing." "It is impossible for men to be moral reformers," he wrote, "and politicians at the same time."

Yet somehow they seemed to be doing it. During the 1840's the "antislavery lobby" in Washington became a real political influence in recruiting support for abolition in and out of Congress. The Congressional controversy over antislavery petitions, engineered by the Washington group, centered national attention on the slavery issue from 1842 to 1846. With giants such as John Quincy Adams and John C. Calhoun locked in debate, the abolitionist claim that Southrons were attempting to "gag the right of petition" received wide publicity in the press. The petition controversy "caused many to think favorably of immediate emancipation," Charles Sumner thought, "who have never before been inclined to think of it."

Antislavery congressmen arrived in Washington in larger numbers after each election — Thaddeus Stevens from Pennsylvania, Owen Lovejoy (brother of the martyred Elijah), and many others. They sponsored bills, raised questions, some important and some trifling, but they kept up the "warm work" started by Giddings, Slade, and the early group. Slavery and its abolition after 1840 became openly debated issues in Congress; the disputes over Texas and the Mexican War, over annexation and slavery extension, were questions that deeply affected the national interest. The Liberty Party failed dismally, but a bloc within the Whig organization took over its work. Antislavery politicians found that they represented a large body of sentiment, and except in Garrisonian portions of New England, a growing number of antislavery voters. The whole drift of the abolitionist crusade was toward politics, partisan politics. As Joshua Leavitt shrewdly observed, abolition was "no longer simply a moral crusade." In setting himself and his society against political action, Garrison set his kind of abolitionism against the trend of the times.

Garrison never regarded political action as anything but folly, maintaining that abolitionists must "use *all* parties and sects . . . but be used by none." By 1848 many of his followers were beginning to doubt, and Garrison seemed willing to relent. When a convention met in Columbus, Ohio, to organize the Free-Soil Party, he remarked in the *Liberator* that while the Free-Soil movement really did not represent "true abolitionism," he would nevertheless refrain from attacking it — though the real issue was still disunion. He would, however, watch the Free-Soilers "with lively interest and give incidental assistance," since "their direction is the same as ours." Quincy, like Garrison, believed that since the Free-Soil Party had "an honest hatred of slavery" it should have the moral support of abolitionists, though they should never abandon "no-government" or disunionist principles. The old Liberty Party, the *Liberator* explained, had really been "the antagonist and not the ally of the antislavery movement . . . officered by deserters." The Free-Soil was not — hence the shift in attitude.

Garrison's sudden change in direction was difficult for all but loyal Garrisonians to follow. Quincy had a hard time explaining the new policy, and reported sadly in October, 1848, that as a result the Free-Soilers had "carried off multitudes of our abolitionists." Garrison was more sanguine, telling Samuel May that the Free-Soil movement was really "unmistakeable proof of the progress we have made, under God, in changing public sentiment." He pointedly avoided any mention of Birney and the earlier political-action group, whose eight years of labor had laid the groundwork for the Free-Soilers.

From 1847 to 1850, suffering from headaches and "weak lungs," Garrison spent the greater part of his time at home. He attended only a few meetings, gave occasional talks, and kept up a voluminous correspondence. Most of his duties he delegated to Quincy and Phillips, who took over responsibility for the *Liberator* and the Massachusetts Antislavery Society. Garrison's home life was as calm as his public life was turbulent. His wife, Helen, was an even-tempered, serene woman who ran a well-ordered household with strength and patience. She bore him seven children, of whom two died in infancy, leaving (in order of age) George Thompson, William Lloyd, Junior, Wendell Phillips, Fanny, and Francis Jackson. In better times Helen had a servant, but through the early years of near-poverty she made all the children's clothes and most of her husband's, performed the necessary household tasks, and cheerfully stretched their scanty income as far as possible. Garrison, in times of financial stress, held to the theory that "the Lord will provide," but it is clear that Helen Garrison gave Him excellent assistance. Though the Garrison home (often called "Abolitionist Hotel") was a free lodging house for itinerant reformers, Mrs. Garrison seemed always equal to the task of maintaining peace and order, or of making food for nine feed twelve or more. Garrison relaxed completely at home. He declaimed poetry, led family singing, and took the children on long walks in the countryside, exclaiming over beautiful views and choosing sites for a hotel, a plan he seems to have had in mind for years.

V I

It Is the Bright Noon of Day

THE CONGRESS that met in December, 1849, was
an able group. Henry Clay was there, and John C. Calhoun; also Daniel Webster, Stephen Douglas, Jefferson
Davis, William H. Seward, A. H. Stephens, and other capable men. Their hope was to find a compromise for the
highly charged question of whether slavery should be allowed to expand, or whether it should be contained within
the South. "The Great Compromiser," Henry Clay of Kentucky, stepped into the breach in January, 1850, with a
series of resolutions designed to effect a reasonable solution. The most important of his suggestions involved admitting California as a free state, placing no restrictions
on slavery in territory gained from the Mexican War, and
instituting a new and stringent Federal fugitive slave law.
The choice was this, said Clay, or disunion, perhaps open
war.

Calhoun spoke for the South, demanding concessions
from the North, asking for recognition of slavery as a permanent national institution. Failing this, he concluded,
"Let the States . . . agree to separate and part in peace."
Webster, the voice of New England, pleaded for union,
compromise, peace — a speech that shocked and angered

the abolitionists, who had considered him their champion. As debate wore on tempers cooled. President Taylor's death brought Millard Fillmore, a born compromiser, into the White House; Calhoun died; Webster's speech had its effect on Northern moderates. Most of Clay's suggestions were incorporated in another bill, passed, and signed by Fillmore into law. The Compromise of 1850 was an accomplished fact. It settled nothing, it satisfied neither North nor South, but it did delay an inevitable decision. And the least important of its provisions — the Fugitive Slave Law — turned out to be the most explosive of all.

By 1850 Garrison's health had improved sufficiently for him to attend the annual May meeting of the American Antislavery Society, held in New York. Abolitionists were angry, and the Compromise of 1850 held the center of attention. Webster's famous Seventh of March speech had already brought bitter protest from New England and the West — "villainy of an unmitigated type," said Garrison, "treachery to the cause of liberty and humanity of the blackest shade." The drawn-out debates in Congress aroused strong feelings and emphasized old antagonisms. Moderates and conservatives in the North, like Webster, wanted sanity, calmness, and reason, not the "irresponsible agitation" of abolitionists.

New York City had never taken kindly to abolitionists, anyway. The national society's annual conventions irritated "merchants, men of business, and men of property," according to James Gordon Bennett's *Herald,* which advised them "to frown down the meetings of these mad people." Garrison, said Bennett, was an enemy of the Union, the Bible, the Sabbath, and Christianity; he advocated "the overthrow of government, a total disrespect of the

Constitution, actual disruption and annihilation of the Union, and a cessation of all order, legal and divine." "Garrison's band of nigger minstrels," the *Sunday Era* thought, ought not to be tolerated in New York. The right of free discussion could hardly be extended so far.

The American Antislavery Society's delegates assembled at Broadway Tabernacle on May 7. Fearing trouble, Gay and Hopper had already appealed to Chief of Police Matsell for protection. Garrison, looking over the crowd, sensed restlessness from the start, and Chairman Francis Jackson hurried through the business session to Garrison's opening speech. Nothing happened until he made a passing reference to slavery and the churches, particularly to slaveholding as practised by Catholics. This brought an immediate response from the floor, from a Tammany politician identified as Captain Isaiah Rynders, a former Hudson River boatman and leader of the Tammany Empire Club. He was a dangerous tough, an expert at inciting mobs. He had already been tried and acquitted for complicity in the MacReady riots of 1849, and less than two months earlier he had been arrested for assault.

Rynders's question was relatively mild. Did not others besides Catholics, he asked, hold slaves? Garrison answered that this was true; neither Episcopalians, Presbyterians, Baptists, nor Methodists could be absolved of guilt. Then Garrison turned to politics, evidently intending to develop the argument that the Federal Government, like the organized churches, offered little hope for the abolitionist. "Jesus," he said, "is the most respectable person in the United States. Jesus sits in the President's chair. Zachary Taylor sits there, which is the same thing, for he believes in Jesus. He believes in war, and in the Jesus who 'gave the Mexicans hell.' "

Garrison's somewhat confused statement brought Rynders running to the platform, shouting "I will not allow you to assail the President of the United States!" Several abolitionists moved toward Rynders and the audience began to shout. Chairman Jackson signaled the Hutchinson Family Singers, who sat near the edge of the platform, to begin a song, but the uproar drowned them out. Rynders stopped on the platform and stood with folded arms, allowing Jackson to restore order and to announce that Rynders would be given time to reply later. Garrison continued without interruption, ending with a resolution that "the antislavery movement, instead of being infidel, in an evil sense (as is falsely alleged) is truly Christian in the primitive sense of the term."

Rynders then announced that his spokesman would reply. The speaker turned out to be a man named Grant who had once worked as a pressman in the *Liberator* offices in Boston. His speech, a rambling, incoherent harangue, seemed to be based on the thesis that Negroes were not men, but animals, and therefore undeserving of freedom. Fred Douglass, seated on the platform, provided a swift and dramatic answer. Rising to his full six feet, Douglass said quietly, "I offer myself for your examination. Am I a man?" and then sat down amid thunderous applause. Rynders had come off distinctly second best. The evening session, featuring speeches by Pillsbury, Foster, and Mrs. Ernestine Rose, attracted only a few jeering spectators.

Rynders's Tammanyites attended the next day's session in force, but Chief Matsell and thirty policemen were on hand. C. C. Burleigh's imposing beard and Garrison's shining baldness attracted a good many ribald comments from the floor, including the suggestion that the one be sheared to make a wig for the other. Though the speakers were occasionally interrupted by "groaning, bellowing, beastly noises, and the foulest language," there was no violence. After the speeches, the Rynders strategy became clear. One of his men offered a resolution that "this meeting does not see sufficient reason for interfering with the domestic institutions of the South . . . and therefore will not countenance fanatical agitation whose aims and ends are the overthrow of churches, a reign of anarchy, a division of interests, the supremacy of a hypocritical atheism, a general amalgamation, and a dissolution of the Union." Jackson ruled the motion out of order, but the Rynders crowd shouted him down. After a hurried conference on the platform, the executive committee announced that the convention was over. The *Liberator* and the *Standard* gave the "mob" wide publicity. The press agreed almost unanimously that harassment of the meeting by Rynders was ill-advised, unworthy, and a threat to free speech. Dr. Furness summarized it well by remarking to Rynders, much to his puzzlement, "How can we ever thank you for what you have done for us?"

The Compromise of 1850, finally passed by Congress in September, gave abolitionism a tremendous boost. Despite the conviction of many Whigs and Democrats that the measures represented a "final settlement of the slavery issue," the Fugitive Slave Act, which formed part of the Compromise, aroused bitter opposition in the North. Abolitionists sponsored protest meetings in Illinois, Connecticut, New York, Ohio, Indiana, Massachusetts, Michigan,

Iowa, and Delaware. Editors throughout the North viewed the law with ire or gloom, and Oliver Johnson reported in the *Antislavery Bugle* that "the papers are filled with discussions of the subject." The abolitionists seized the trend of opinion and capitalized on it. Garrison correctly estimated that the 1850 act swayed more Northern neutrals toward tolerance of abolitionism than any event since Lovejoy's death. When Ralph Waldo Emerson, who was not ordinarily moved by passing events, wrote curtly in his journal, "By God, I will not obey it!" he spoke for thousands of moderate Northerners. To the abolitionists themselves the Fugitive Slave Act was a rallying point away from all the schisms and disagreements which plagued the movement. On this issue political actionists, disunionists, nonvoters, and nonresistants could unite.

Abolitionists argued that the fugitive slave provisions of the Compromise were contrary to "higher law," and therefore not to be obeyed. Many nonabolitionists felt the same. "We feel that there is a law of right," said Joshua Giddings in the House, "of justice, of freedom, implanted in the breast of every intelligent human being, that bids him look with scorn upon this libel on all that is called the law." Hundreds of Northerners, who had long looked with distaste on abolition, agreed that the law must not be obeyed, and gave open or moral support to violations of it.

After 1850 nearly every year had its fugitive slave case, each eminently newsworthy and highly publicized — Henry Long in New York, William Crafts and his wife in Boston, the famous "Jerry Rescue" in Syracuse, Shadrach and Sims of Boston, William Parker in Philadelphia, "Peggy's Children" in Cincinnati, Glover in Wisconsin, and Anthony Burns in Boston. Eighty-one major cases

marked the decade, and each had an effect on public opinion. A correspondent reminded Oliver Johnson how little
antislavery sentiment there once was in Cass County,
Michigan. "It has greatly changed since," he wrote. "Our
citizens side almost with entire unanimity with the poor
captives and fugitives, and there is deep feeling on the
subject." Cass County's reaction was typical. The shift of
Northern opinion took concrete form in the state "personal liberty" laws passed after 1850, intended to rectify
the violations of civil rights in the Federal law and sometimes in direct conflict with it. Eleven Northern states prohibited citizens or law officers from aiding in the execution
of the Federal statute. Five prohibited the use of public
buildings for any purpose which might aid the master or
his agent, while eight provided defense for fugitives at
public expense. That these laws were passed in every free
state except Ohio and Indiana indicated the cumulative
effect of the controversy on Northern opinion.

The Fugitive Slave Law also gave a powerful impetus to
the "underground railroad." Some machinery for the aid
of escaping slaves had existed since the 1830's, but after
1850 the system expanded tremendously. The British abolition acts had made Canada a haven for fugitives, and the
personal liberty laws of Northern states made recovery difficult. Disobedience to the despised Federal law became,
to many Northerners, a patriotic, Christian act, and a
steady stream of escaped slaves ran through communities
that twenty years earlier had mobbed abolitionist agents.
By 1852 it was boasted that a slave could be run from a
border state into Canada in forty-eight hours; invitations
and instructions were openly printed in antislavery papers.
The underground railroad did not appreciably weaken

slavery, but it strengthened antislavery feeling in the North by making the fugitive the object of compassion and by underlining the dangers to human liberty. The Dred Scott case, when it came in 1857, seemed to many in the North, abolitionist and anti-abolitionist alike, simply the last act of "a great conspiracy" against freedom and "a direct denial of the Declaration of Independence."

Northern attitudes changed fast. Nonabolitionist editors, Garrison noted after 1850, "now severally treat abolitionists with respect . . . and refer to their doctrines and measures without misrepresentation." George Thompson, who arrived in Boston for a tour late that year, was pleasantly surprised by his New England audiences, who no longer threw eggs or threatened him with the tar kettle. Bronson Alcott wrote in his diary that "extremes are getting less extreme. . . . Even Phillips and Garrison and Pillsbury are listened to with some respect." "I respect the Antislavery society," Emerson said. "It is the Cassandra that has foretold all that has befallen, fact for fact, years ago." Garrison too was surprised to find that respectable New York and Boston papers now printed extracts from his speeches, occasionally publishing one in full.

For the first time since 1831, Garrison and the *Liberator* had respectable company. Had it not been for his natural independence of nature, his refusal to brook disagreement, and his persistent adherence to issues only distantly related to abolition, Garrison might have become after 1850 the national antislavery leader he claimed and hoped to be. But disunion, women's rights, nonresistance, "no-government," and anticlericalism kept him and his followers on a separate, though parallel, path to that of the main body of antislavery activity.

Wendell Phillips, not Garrison, emerged as the real leader of New England abolitionism, placed there by his own golden tongue and the Fugitive Slave Law. Phillips thundered against slavery from a hundred platforms, lashed at the "slavecatchers" in the columns of the *Liberator* and the *Standard,* and poured abuse on hapless Daniel Webster. When Boston citizens organized a group of vigilantes to aid runaway slaves, Garrison, in deference to his nonresistance principles, was not asked to serve. Phillips, on the other hand, dominated its executive committee. When Josiah Quincy called a protest meeting in Faneuil Hall, it was Phillips, not Garrison, who whipped the crowd into a near-frenzy with his oratory. "Garrison was thrown into the background," Archibald Grimké wrote later. "Forcible resistance to the black bill was now obedience to God," and Garrison was a nonresistant.

Meanwhile, the rise of Charles Sumner gave abolitionists another political hero. Sumner, who helped to found the Free-Soil Party, entered the Senate in 1851 and soon became the most violent and powerful antagonist of slavery in Washington. By mid-decade, Phillips and Sumner were the twin spearheads of New England abolitionism. People thought of Garrison as an elder statesman in the movement, sincere, eloquent, but a little old-fashioned.

Garrison's health, it was true, was not strong, and his finances, always dubious, were drained dry by frequent illnesses. For twenty years he had existed on a small, irregular income from lecture fees and the *Liberator,* augmented by occasional purses collected by admirers. In 1850 his friends began a drive for a larger fund, which in a few years was sizable enough to purchase for him a house in Boston's Dix Place. Free from financial worries for the first time, he threw himself back into the abolitionist controversy with renewed energy. His long period of rest had worked no changes; he was still unpredictable, uncompromising, and independent, leading skirmishes in several directions at once. In 1852 he involved himself in an argument with the supporters of Louis Kossuth, the Hungarian patriot who visited the United States. Kossuth's determination to remain neutral on the slavery issue disappointed Garrison, who censured him publicly for accepting donations from slaveholders. The current interest in spiritualism found Garrison in another controversy over the authenticity of spirit rappings. After attending a séance held by one of the Fox sisters, he came away almost convinced by "messages" from the departed shade of Isaac Hopper, and from the ghost of Jesse Hutchinson of the singing family, who beat time on the table and patted Garrison's head.

In March, 1852, Harriet Beecher Stowe's *Uncle Tom's Cabin* appeared in book form, and Garrison reviewed it in the *Liberator*. The novel had already been serialized in Bailey's *National Era,* a paper Garrison sedulously avoided, and his review of the book that was to sell more than a million copies within a year was a masterpiece of misunderstanding. Garrison admitted the emotional power of her story, but preferred to read it as a novel that "triumphantly exemplifies the nature, tendency, and results of CHRISTIAN NON-RESISTANCE." Its effectiveness as abolitionist propaganda evidently escaped him, for he spent nearly his entire column on a discussion of Uncle

Tom as a nonresistant, closing with a criticism of Mrs. Stowe's "objectionable sentiment respecting colonization, which we regret to see."

When the book sold like wildfire, Phillips tried to take advantage of the opportunities that Garrison had missed. It was perfectly clear, in Phillips's opinion, that the story could never have been written "had not Garrison developed the facts, and never would have succeeded had he not created readers and purchasers." That Harriet Stowe knew Garrison only by reputation, and that she had been more probably inspired by Weld's *Slavery As It Is,* bothered Phillips not at all. After reading Garrison's review she wrote him a letter expressing her admiration for him while admitting at the same time her fears of his "infidelity." "What I fear," she wrote, "is that it will take from poor Uncle Tom his Bible, and give him nothing to take its place." Garrison's reply reassured her of his Christianity, but Wright's *Liberator* pieces on the authenticity of Scripture continued to bother her. The *Liberator* did not seem to her to display "a cautious and reverential spirit," and Phillips was worried lest her fears of "The Prince of New England Infidelity" drive abolitionism's most effective novelist into Tappan's group. She visited Garrison twice, but neither seemed quite able to understand what the other was trying to do.

Garrison's crusade for disunion continued to make news during the 1850's. The course of events convinced him, he wrote, of what he had always believed — abolition could never be attained by political means. Both major parties were solidly proslavery; the passage of the Kansas-Nebraska bill, the Kansas troubles, the election of Buchanan in 1856, and the Republican defeats of that year simply proved to him the folly of political action. "So far as national politics are concerned we are beaten," he wrote. "There's no hope — the sky was never so dark. Our Union, all confess, must sever finally on this question." Disunion, a peaceful separation of North from South, was the only logical answer to the disorder of contemporary politics. His nonresistant principles would not allow him to approve Beecher's and Parker's plans for sending armed emigrants to Kansas, and his no-voting beliefs prevented him from finding allies in the new Republican Party, whose aims he termed "feeble and indefinite." The Republicans deserved support — "If we had a million votes to bestow, we should cast them all for the Republicans" — but the solution to the slavery problem lay in principles, not votes. Horace Greeley, who found Garrison's editorials on politics confusing, asked him directly whether or not he intended to vote, and if so, how. He did not intend to, Garrison replied, for the Republican Party "goes for perpetuating the Union as it is — we are for its immediate dissolution." True abolitionism meant still but one thing, No Union with Slaveholders!

Garrison's uncompromising refusal to tolerate political action nearly killed the Massachusetts and the American Antislavery Societies, which lost members right and left. Despite Garrison's warnings, "voting abolitionists" almost to a man went into the Republican Party, to become its "radical wing," though Burleigh, Pillsbury, Wright, Phillips, Foster, May, and others of the faithful stayed at Garrison's side, with a few new enlistments such as Thomas Wentworth Higginson, Francis Bird, and Daniel Mann. All the Garrisonian societies went on record in favor of immediate disunion, and all exhorted their members not to vote for any candidate or party. Resolutions calling for dissolution of the Union were approved by every yearly convention of the Massachusetts and American societies from 1850 to 1861. This was "the grand vital issue," Garrison told the national society in 1854, and Phillips echoed him, "The sooner the Union goes to pieces, the better!"

Two months later, speaking at a Fourth of July celebration at Framingham, Garrison emphasized his belief in somewhat spectacular fashion. After a violent attack on the Constitution, he drew from his pocket copies of the document itself, of the Fugitive Slave Law, and of several court decisions on fugitive slave cases, touched a match to them, and then ground the ashes under his heel, exclaiming, "So perish all compromises with tyranny — and let the people say Amen!" The Framingham incident was too strong for some of his adherents to accept, so Garrison explained in the *Liberator* that "I burnt a PRO-SLAVERY constitution, in my judgment . . . , and therefore was faithful to the slave in so doing." The Free-Soil Party in Massachusetts, however, hastily announced that it opposed "sectionalism, secession, and disunion," disclaimed Garrisonian support, and warned Free-soilers against him.

Garrison's disunion talk led to the suspicion in abolitionist circles that he was more interested in breaking up the Union than in freeing the slaves. His remarks at meeting after meeting seemed to justify that belief. It became an obsession with him, an issue wider than abolition, one that at bottom involved basic Christian as well as humanitarian principles. At the 1857 meeting of the Massachusetts Society, Phillips, Garrison, Quincy, Higginson, and Thomas Earle of Worcester framed a resolution calling for a state disunion convention to meet in Worcester the following week to "consider the practicability, probability, and expediency of a separation between the Free and the Slave States." It was a huge failure, "nothing more than a Garrisonian meeting," Garrison wrote, "with exception of a few quondam Republicans." Letters from prominent politicians, solicited by the steering committee, were uniformly disappointing. Charles Francis Adams, Joshua Giddings, Amasa Walker, Henry Wilson, and others in Congress gave guarded, noncommittal statements that left Garrison unsatisfied. Somewhat unenthusiastically the convention heard speeches, passed the proper resolutions, and appointed a seven-man committee (headed by Higginson) to direct a disunionist movement in Massachusetts.

The fiasco at Worcester dampened the disunionists' spirits, but not enough to dissuade them from another attempt to organize. The Western Antislavery Society, following Garrison's policy, had already petitioned the Ohio legislature to withdraw that state from the Union, and both the *Liberator* and the *Antislavery Bugle,* its Ohio counterpart, editorialized on the necessity of an alliance between Eastern and Western disunionists. Higginson, Phillips, Garrison, Mann, and Bird issued a call for a national disunion convention, to be held in Cleveland in the autumn of 1857. In the midst of their preparations, the panic of 1857 struck, and the organizing committee reluctantly postponed the Cleveland meeting. An informal convention, attended chiefly by agents from the American, Massachusetts, and Western societies, did meet in October, heard a few speeches, and disbanded. No attempt was ever made to renew the call.

As a matter of fact, events after 1856 moved far too

swiftly for William Lloyd Garrison. His simple theory of peaceful separation of slave and free states was if anything too conservative for the younger, more militant abolitionists like Phillips and Higginson, who advocated disunion even at the cost of war. Garrison's opposition to political action, set against the meteoric rise of the Republican Party, alienated many of his supporters, while his continuous emphasis on abolition as a moral crusade — and nothing else — seemed old-fashioned and impractical. At the annual meetings of the New England Convention and the American Antislavery Society in 1858, Garrison found among the delegates an aggressive, politically-minded spirit that saddened him, and he scolded them for it. Abolition, he reminded them, was "baptized in the spirit of peace," and he regretted to see it "growing more and more warlike." "Moral power," he continued, "will depart from the movement in proportion as the spirit of violence grows." But T. W. Higginson, already conferring secretly with John Brown, openly disagreed: "Is slavery destined, as it began in blood, so to end? Seriously and solemnly I say, it seems as if it were." Theodore Parker, another confidant of Brown's, thought the time had passed when the slavery question "could have been settled without bloodshed."

Garrison knew nothing of Brown's plot, nor of the complicity in it of any of the New England abolitionists. His nonresistant views were too well known to have made him a likely conspirator, and Higginson, Parker, Sanborn, and the others kept it from him. Garrison and Brown met twice, once in 1857 at Parker's house, where they argued about pacifism, and again in early 1859 at the New England Antislavery Convention, where Brown was heard to mutter after hearing the speeches, "These men are all talk; what is needed is action, action!"

Garrison heard the news from Harpers Ferry on October 19, 1859, and in the next issue of the *Liberator* printed an account of the "misguided, wild, and apparently insane, though disinterested and well-intentioned effort by insurrection to emancipate the slaves of Virginia." In subsequent issues he reprinted extracts from other papers on Brown's trial and execution without much comment, except to repeat his disapproval of the "war spirit" that had led Brown astray. He did consent to join the executive committee of the American Antislavery Society in asking that Brown's hanging day, December 2, 1859, be made a day of national mourning. Later, at the Tremont Temple meeting in commemoration of Brown, he read Brown's address to the court movingly and sincerely. At the same time Garrison made his position on the Harpers Ferry affair crystal clear. He was "a peace man," he said, but it was no violation of his principles to "wish success to any slave insurrection in the South." He could never agree with Brown's method, though he could approve his aim. "In firing his gun," Garrison told the Tremont Temple crowd, "John Brown has merely told us what time of day it is. It is high noon, thank God."

Garrison spent most of the year 1860 resting in the White Mountains, hoping to rid himself of recurring lung trouble. He sent in his regular weekly column to the *Liberator,* though he left the paper itself almost completely in the hands of young C. K. Whipple, who joined him as editorial assistant in 1857. He also edited the *New Reign of Terror,* a pamphlet reprinting accounts of mobs and attacks on the abolitionist press, and published it with funds willed to the abolitionists by Charles Hovey of Boston. Most of his time he spent in clipping newspapers (a habit he maintained through his life) and in writing letters to abolitionists and congressmen. Secession talk in the South (and papers were filled with it in 1860) encouraged him to believe that disunion was closer than ever; the split in the Democratic presidential convention he hailed as "the most cheering sign in years." The failure of the Republicans at their convention to take a strong disunionist stand disappointed him. How could the Republican Party, he asked, resist the extension of slavery on the one hand because it was a crime, and then on the other support it where it existed because it was constitutional? The Republican platform seemed weak, and the nomination of Lincoln unwise. Seward, he thought, would have been a better choice.

Garrison refrained from pre-election comments on Lincoln, but Phillips was less charitable. "Who is this huckster in politics?" Phillips asked. "Who is this who does not know whether he has got any opinions about slavery?" And he sent the *Liberator* an abusive article, entitled "Abraham Lincoln, the Slave-Hound of Illinois." The tone of Phillips's attack worried Whipple; Garrison was reluctant to publish it unless Phillips signed it and took full responsibility, which he did. The results of the election Garrison received with only temperate joy. Phillips thought Lincoln better than nothing, remarking with confused logic, "Lincoln is *in place,* but Garrison is *in power.*"

Neither Garrison nor Phillips expected a great deal from Lincoln. "If he *is* six feet four inches high," Garrison told Oliver Johnson, "he is only a dwarf in mind." The secession conventions in the South that followed the election made Lincoln's attempt to save the Union, in Garrison's opinion, "simply idiotic." He feared, too, that the new President might succeed in working out some compromise with the Southern states that might preserve the Union, but would also preserve slavery. Garrison did not attend the annual meeting of the Massachusetts Antislavery Society held in January, 1861, but Phillips and Higginson attacked Lincoln so violently that the Boston police finally requested the society to close its meeting to avoid a riot. Garrison's own remarks in the *Liberator* were more temperate, but none the less critical. He kept up a steady stream of articles from his haven in the White Mountains, exhorting Lincoln to let the errant sisters go. "The people of the North should recognize the fact that the UNION IS DISSOLVED, and act accordingly," he advised the President. "Let there be a convention of the Free States, called to organize an independent government on free and just principles, and let them say to the Slave States . . . 'Organize your own confederacy, if you will, based upon violence, tyranny, and blood, and relieve us from all responsibility for your evil course!' "

The bombardment of Sumter, and Lincoln's call for troops, brought Garrison to the President's support at once. Lincoln's determination to crush rebellion, thought Garrison, called for rejoicing among abolitionists. Yet the fact that the South had seceded placed Garrison and other disunionists in an awkward position. After preaching disunion for more than a decade, they recognized that to allow the slave states to secede simply meant that slavery would continue to flourish in the South without hindrance. As a disunionist himself, how could Garrison challenge the right of the South to secede? And as a nonresistant pacifist, how could he justify a war to prevent that secession?

Garrison took two long editorials in the *Liberator* to explain his stand. All reasonable means, he said, had been exhausted to persuade the South to abolish slavery; instead, the South had attempted to extend it. Lincoln's determination to prevent the extension of slavery did not constitute sufficient reason for secession, which was justifiable only for causes such as those listed in the Declaration of Independence. The South therefore had neither a moral nor a legal right to withdraw from the Union. Phillips, who saw matters in much the same light, now praised Lincoln as fulsomely as he had attacked him bitterly three months before. Abolitionists, the *Liberator* announced, must do nothing to divert "the mighty current of popular feeling" in the President's behalf; the American Antislavery Society's annual meetings would be canceled until further notice. "Let us all stand aside," Garrison wrote Johnson, "when the North is rushing like a tornado in the right direction." The approaching war would either "achieve the goal of universal emancipation, or else a separation between the free and slaveholding states in accordance with the principle, No Union with Slaveholders." In either case, the abolitionists won.

Garrison's support of the war raised questions about his peace principles, particularly when the *Liberator*, breathing fire against the Confederacy, displayed unusual belligerence. Garrison therefore undertook to explain that his principles were as "beneficent and glorious as ever . . .

neither disproved nor modified" by events. The fact that
he supported the Federal Government in time of war
seemed to him to bear no relation to his nonresistance. In
a war between justice and injustice, any "peace man"
might wish success to the right cause without compromising his personal principles. If Lincoln, Congress, and the
North believed it necessary to prevent secession by force,
he explained, they must be true to their own beliefs.
Theirs were not his, he admitted, but "the worst thing
they can do is to be recreant to their own convictions in
such a crisis as this."

The Garrisonians waited hopefully throughout 1861 for
Lincoln to free the slaves. When nothing happened, Phillips, Foster, Johnson, and Higginson framed angry resolutions at abolitionist meetings, while Garrison pleaded with
them to be patient. "It is no time," he counseled Johnson,
"for minute criticism of Lincoln. All our sympathies must
be with the Government. There must be no needless turning of popular violence upon ourselves by any false step of
our own." When the war was done, he cautioned Foster,
then "is the time to criticize, reprove, and condemn." He
wrote to Thompson in England, asking him to rally British support to the President, and despite his dislike of what
he called Lincoln's "new doctrine of Republican conserv-
atism," Thompson agreed to help. At his urging the
London Emancipation Society distributed thousands of
pamphlets explaining the issues of the American war, con-
siderably easing Northern propaganda efforts abroad.

But Garrison's faith in Lincoln frequently faltered.
The President's oft-expressed determination to restore the
Union — with or without slavery — seemed to Garrison
doubly false and deluded. The old Union, he wrote, "is *non*

est inventus, and its restoration, with its proslavery compromises, well-nigh impossible." Disunion was a permanent fact. The old motto No UNION WITH SLAVEHOLDERS!
disappeared from the *Liberator,* replaced by PROCLAIM
LIBERTY THROUGHOUT THE LAND, TO ALL THE INHABITANTS
THEREOF. "Blessed be to God," Garrison told the New England Convention, "that the 'covenant with death' has been
annulled, and that the 'agreement with hell' no longer
stands."

Yet to the New England abolitionists Lincoln seemed
strangely slow-moving and reluctant. Phillips railed
against him, in the *Liberator* and from the platform, as
"that first-rate second-rate man" whose "milk-livered administration" was guilty of "conducting the war, at present, with the purpose of saving slavery." General Fré-
mont's order freeing the slaves in Missouri made Garrison
and Phillips cheer; Lincoln's swift cancellation of the order chilled and depressed them. If Lincoln "had been a
traitor," said Phillips, "he could not have worked better to
strengthen one side, and hazard the success of the other."
The President, Garrison privately told Johnson, "has evidently not a drop of antislavery blood in his veins, and
he seems incapable of uttering a humane or a generous
sentiment respecting the enslaved millions in our land."

As the war continued and no proclamation of emancipation appeared from Washington, Garrison's criticisms
grew sharper. He circulated petitions asking for immediate emancipation, exhorted the antislavery societies to protest to Congress, and addressed editorials to Lincoln in the
Liberator. "To refuse to deliver these captive millions who
are now legally in your power," he told Lincoln, "is tanta-
mount to the crime of their original enslavement, and

their blood shall a righteous God require at your hands."
At the same time, Garrison refrained (as Phillips, Gerrit
Smith, and others did not) from violent and intemperate
public attacks on the President. In private letters he might
write, as he did to his wife, that Lincoln was "nothing better than a wet rag," but in the *Liberator* his criticism,
though edged, was respectful. He wrote: "I am willing to
believe . . . that there is some ground for hesitancy, as a
mere matter of political expediency." Garrison did not
join Samuel Gridley Howe, Francis Bird, Franklin Sanborn, Moncure Conway, and others who formed an Emancipation League in Boston to agitate for immediate emancipation. As a greater concession to expediency, he agreed
to insert in a petition to the President, drawn up in late
1861, a clause recommending Federal compensation to
loyal Southerners who freed their slaves. On the level of
principle, he found reason to quarrel with the President,
but on the level of practical politics he recognized Lincoln's problems. Phillips's attacks on Lincoln he regarded
as excessive, and he advised Oliver Johnson, then editing
the *National Antislavery Standard*, to weigh his editorial
words carefully. "I have always believed," he wrote Johnson (strange advice from the one-time advocate of "harsh
language") "that the antislavery cause has aroused against
it a great deal of uncalled-for hostility, in consequence of
extravagances of speech and want of tact and good judgment. . . ."

Garrison's determination to "err on the side of charitable judgment" was illustrated by his most important public address during the period, "The Abolitionists and
Their Relation to the War," given at Cooper Institute in
New York in early 1862. A two-hour speech, later re-

printed and distributed in pamphlet form, it was a careful, temperate vindication of the motives and methods of the abolitionists. Abolitionism, Garrison declared, was not responsible for the war, nor was it guilty of fomenting secession. Emancipation of the slaves, he explained, was essential to victory, peace, and preservation of the Union after peace. As for his familiar motto, now gone from the *Liberator,* he remarked, "I had no idea that I should live to see death and hell secede," but such being the case, "I am now with the Government, to enable it to constitutionally stop the further ravages of death, and to extinguish the flames of hell forever." From the war, he hoped, there would arise a new Union, free and indissoluble, and within it a new South "redeemed from the curse of slavery . . . a garden of God."

Garrison's Cooper Institute speech attracted a great deal of favorable attention, so much so that the executive committee of the American Antislavery Society suggested that Garrison and Phillips continue to lecture. A successful tour, they hoped, might arouse sufficient sentiment for emancipation to force Lincoln's hand. There was another advantage too; the society and its auxiliaries might be able to discontinue some of their agencies and publications, leaving only Garrison, Phillips, the *Standard,* and the *Liberator* for its strained treasury to support. A suggestion that perhaps the two newspapers might merge, saving still more money, Garrison quickly scotched. He did, however, consent to travel through Massachusetts and New York State in the spring of 1862, while Phillips went to Washington, where he was received with open arms by the Radical Republicans in Congress.

Abolitionist delegations called on Lincoln almost every week through the spring and summer of 1862, all of them urging a proclamation of emancipation. Phillips had an inconclusive interview with him. Garrison drafted a memorial to him, which Oliver Johnson personally presented to the President, who received it with what the *Liberator* called "puerile, absurd, illogical, impertinent, and untimely" remarks. Nevertheless Garrison continued to defend Lincoln's temporizing policy. In the face of Phillips's bitter arraignment of Lincoln at the annual meeting of the Massachusetts society, Garrison pleaded that the President's conduct of the war furnished "high ground for encouragement," though he seemed "unnecessarily timid and deserving of rebuke." The society failed to pass any resolutions of censure, but there was strong feeling that Garrison's attitude was too charitable, too conservative, too compromising. The rift between Garrison and Phillips was quite visible after the spring of 1862.

The truth probably was that after thirty years as a dissenter Garrison found it pleasant to be on the winning side and to reap the rewards of being right. The nation had finally come to Garrison, and while it had not come to him so completely as he had hoped, it seemed to him that for once he and majority opinion were at least running on parallel roads. As the elder statesman and respected oracle of the original antislavery movement, he commanded the respect of Congressmen, editors, public leaders, and even of the President of the United States himself. Victory was close, very close. Garrison wanted no applecarts upset.

It was also true that the personnel and temper of the abolitionist movement had changed since Garrison first began his crusade. Garrison's time, some of the younger men believed, was almost past; it was time now to look for other leaders. By 1862 Wendell Phillips was the person to whom the antislavery movement looked for its wartime leadership. During the winter of 1861–1862 more than fifty thousand people heard him speak, and more than five million read his speeches. His lectures attracted immense audiences, Republican papers hung on his words, Congressmen flocked to his hotel when he visited Washington. What Phillips had to say about the war was direct and simple, and he said it effectively. Free the slaves; crush the South; annihilate the slaveholding oligarchy; destroy Southern society and rebuild it on the sturdy foundation of the freed Negro, the farmer, the artisan. This was exactly what Thaddeus Stevens of Pennsylvania, or Henry Wilson and Charles Sumner of Massachusetts, or any of the Radical Republican opponents of Lincoln were saying, though often not so eloquently as Phillips. Garrison's message of caution, tact, patience, and expediency did not fit the mood of a nation at war.

On September 23, 1862, Lincoln justified Garrison's faith. On that day the President issued the preliminary Emancipation Proclamation, promising that "All persons held as slaves within any State, or designated part of a State" whose population was in rebellion on January 1, 1863, would be "then, henceforth, and forever free." There were, Garrison noted in the *Liberator,* certain flaws in the proclamation — notably its offer to assist in colonizing "persons of African descent, with their consent, upon this continent or elsewhere" — but nevertheless Lincoln's act was of "immense historic consequence." Still it was too bad, he told his daughter, that "the President can do noth-

ing for freedom in a direct manner, but only by circum-
locution and delay."

But as January 1, 1863, approached, Garrison's spirits
rose and his doubts dissolved. He was in Medford, Massachusetts, dedicating a statue of John Brown, when the news
of the finalizing of the Emancipation Act reached Boston
amid wild ringing of church bells. The next day's *Liberator* uttered his "Glory, Hallelujah." "Thirty years ago," he
told a joyful victory meeting of the Massachusetts society,
"it was midnight with the antislavery cause; now it is the
bright noon of day, with the sun shining in his meridian
splendor." For Garrison, the thirty-year battle was almost
done.

The Emancipation Proclamation fixed William Lloyd
Garrison's place in history. He and those who cleaved to
him through thirty years of agitation accepted Lincoln's
proclamation as final justification of their work. From
1831 to 1840 Garrison and his followers had gone largely
unheard, condemned when they were heard, suffering all
the indignities and frustrations of unpopular minorities.
After 1840, events conspired to Garrison's aid. He
preached disunion, warned of the machinations of the
"slavepower conspiracy," attacked slavery as immoral and
inhumane, and predicted a war to come between freedom
and tyranny. After Texas and 1846, Garrisonian disunion
did not look quite so inflammatory to respectable men.
The Fugitive Slave Law of 1850 did seem unjust and barbaric, in conflict with that "higher law" of conscience that
Garrison had long claimed as his own. When the sheriff's
men marched black Anthony Burns in manacles to the
train that took him back to slavery, the silent Boston

throng that watched felt that perhaps Garrison was right in refusing to compromise with evil. Three thousand clergymen signed a petition opposing the Kansas-Nebraska bill; the petition said in almost the same terms what Garrison had preached for a quarter of a century. This time, when Garrison made a speech against the bill, the New York *Times* printed it in full. The *Liberator* said that the Constitution was a proslavery document; the Dred Scott decision looked very much like another Garrisonian warning come true. Disunion came, death and hell seceded; the proslavery South "conspired" against the free North — perhaps not quite in the way Garrison predicted, and not for the same reasons, but close enough. Abolition won, and Garrison, who had claimed its ownership for thirty years, became the convenient public symbol of its victory.

V I I

To Finish It Up

GARRISON'S LIFE after January, 1863, was a long
anticlimax. He was fifty-eight, tired from years of overwork, and in ill health. Readers of the *Liberator* sensed
the change in him; the paper's tone was softer, less belligerent, as if its editor were content to drift with the tide
of events. He did not hesitate to criticize when criticism
seemed deserved, but the familiar bite was gone from his
prose.

In the spring of 1863, young George Thompson Garrison accepted a lieutenant's commission in the Fifty-fourth
Massachusetts, one of two Negro regiments formed in Massachusetts. His father did not object. "I have nothing but
praise to give you," he told his son, "that you have been
faithful to your highest convictions, and taking your life in
your hands, are willing to lay it down . . . in the cause of
freedom, and for the suppression of slavery and rebellion."
Much as he disliked the apparatus of war, Garrison visited
at the Readville training camp regularly, and when the
Fifty-fourth marched to the wharf to embark for action, he
stood in the rain to watch. As the Negro soldiers swung
smartly down State Street, Garrison suddenly realized he
stood at the corner of Wilson's Lane, the spot over which

he had been dragged by the mob, a rope about his waist, in 1835.

Abolitionist conventions met in wartime, but the spark had gone out of them. Only six New Englanders appeared at the American Antislavery Society convention in the spring of 1863, and the chief items of business at such meetings seemed to be the customary resolutions of advice to Lincoln. George Thompson suggested that Garrison tour England to enlist support for the Union cause. He refused, pleading his own and his wife's ill-health. Mrs. Garrison's condition grew worse through 1863, and her husband spent more and more time at home. In December she suffered a stroke that left her partially paralyzed.

Relations between Garrison and Phillips remained cool. Phillips attacked Lincoln's proposed plan of reconstruction sharply. His own, explained in dozens of speeches, resembled more and more that of Thad Stevens and the Radicals in Congress. Lincoln's Reconstruction Message, read to Congress in December, 1863, evoked protests from Phillips; Garrison merely remarked that "Mr. Lincoln's magnanimity is weakness." Phillips's program was direct and simple: "Confiscate and divide the lands of the rebels, extend the right of suffrage as broadly as possible to whites and blacks, let the Federal Constitution prohibit slavery throughout the Union, and forbid the States to make any distinction among their citizens on account of color or race." The problem, as Phillips saw it, was to annihilate not only a system but a state of mind. Lincoln's message, soft and forgiving, appeared to him "neither wise, safe, nor feasible," and the President himself a man "of loathsome ignorance," unfit to lead the Negro to freedom.

Garrison did not agree. Lincoln, he reminded Phillips,

could not afford to outdistance public opinion. Since the
right of suffrage constitutionally belonged to the States,
Lincoln could not be censured for his reluctance to violate
"a universal rule" by forcing a Federal edict upon them.
In thirty years of abolitionist agitation, he recalled, the
matter of votes for the freed Negro had never been a vital
issue (this was not strictly true) nor had it formed any essential part of the abolitionist argument. Furthermore, he
explained to Professor Francis Newman of London, to give
the freed Negro a vote immediately was not at all practica-
ble, "according to the laws of development and progress."
A Negro could be translated from auction block to freeman at once; to place him before a ballot box, invested
with all political rights and immunities, was a different
thing. The freed slave was not ready, in Garrison's opinion, to manage his own political affairs. Better wait with
Lincoln for "a general preparation of feeling and sentiment," until "colorophobia" began to disappear and until
the South itself was prepared to grant "wealth, eminence,
distinction, and official station" to the black man.

The open break between Garrison and Phillips finally
came at the annual winter meeting of the Massachusetts
Antislavery Society in 1864, at which Phillips introduced
a resolution condemning the Lincoln administration for
"being ready to sacrifice the interest and the honor of the
North to secure a sham peace." Garrison objected. "True,"
he replied, Lincoln was "open to criticism for his slow-
ness" and needed "spurring on to yet more decisive action," but Phillips's language implied that the President
was "willing to do a base thing for a base end . . . a very
grave charge." Nevertheless Garrison's proposal to amend

the resolution lost by a narrow margin. The two men patched it up with complimentary speeches, but the fact remained that Phillips had won the first test of strength and that he, not Garrison, controlled the majority of votes in the Massachusetts society.

The contest between old leader and new one continued through the election year of 1864. Garrison favored Lincoln's renomination; Phillips strenuously opposed it. At successive meetings of the Massachusetts Antislavery Society, the American Antislavery Society, and the New England Antislavery Convention the two men fenced over resolutions. Lincoln, Phillips charged, sought "to adjourn the battle from cannon shot to forum, from Grant to Senate House, and to leave the poisoned remnants of the slave system for a quarter century to come." Lincoln intended "to make as little change as possible; touch slavery the last thing; touch it as little as possible!" "The crisis is too solemn to justify heat or dogmatism," Garrison replied. "A thousand incidental errors and blunders are easily borne with on the part of him who, at one blow, severed the chains of three million three hundred thousand slaves — thus virtually abolishing the whole system." This time Garrison won, for the American Antislavery Society and the New England Convention did not adopt Phillips's hot-worded resolutions of censure. But Phillips did split the Garrisonian phalanx: Pillsbury, Stephen and Abby Foster, and a few other of Garrison's old friends voted against him. Phillips refused to concede defeat and went on to accept, for the first time in his life, a place in politics. Elected a delegate to the Republican State Convention, he carried his attack on Lincoln to the convention floor, but to no avail, since the meeting endorsed Lincoln's renomination.

Garrison's support of the President embittered Phillips, but he kept his criticisms in private. "I should rather have severed my right hand," he told a friend, "than write pro-Lincoln articles for the *Liberator*" as Garrison did.

The Republican (National Union) Convention met in Baltimore in June, with Garrison in attendance as a spectator in the gallery. He was extremely pleased at Lincoln's nomination and with the Republican platform, which seemed to him "a full endorsement of all the abolition 'fanaticism' and 'incendiarism' with which I stood branded for so many years." Theodore Tilton, editor of the New York *Independent*, who accompanied Garrison to Baltimore, wrote that at his appearance "all hats went off, all hands were thrust in welcome, and all hospitable manners shown" to the man who, thirty-four years earlier, served a jail sentence in that very city for speaking out against slavery. The one-time "fanatical, heretical, and incendiary gentleman" was welcomed as a "modest and meek-minded conservative" by the delegates. His reception, Garrison wrote his wife, was "a complete vindication" of all he stood for.

Garrison stayed on in Baltimore for a few days, for the city was filled with memories. He visited the courtroom in which he had been sentenced in the Todd case, and Judge Hugh Bond, a staunch Unionist, looked up the faded indictment and read it aloud to him. The old jail, with Garrison's sonnets on the wall, was gone, much to his disappointment, although eight of the jurors who had convicted him were still alive, and the judge jokingly offered to call them together for another trial. With Bond and Tilton he traveled on to Washington, where Senator Henry Wilson of Massachusetts had arranged an interview with Lincoln for him. After a brief, pleasant chat with the President, Garrison visited Stanton, whom he found full of "a thorough-going antislavery spirit and purpose." Then as Sumner's guest he attended a session of the Senate, where the Republican Senators thronged to meet him. The next day he and Tilton spent more than an hour with Lincoln. He hoped, the President said, that a constitutional amendment abolishing slavery would soon pass; he had great difficulties to contend with, and he wanted to get the amendment through Congress swiftly in case he failed of re-election. The interview reassured Garrison immensely. "There is no mistake about it in regard to Mr. Lincoln's desire to do all he can . . . to uproot slavery," he wrote to his wife, "and give fair play to the emancipated. I was very much pleased with his spirit."

Lincoln's election and the adoption of the Thirteenth Amendment by Congress convinced Garrison that the abolition crusade was over. The news from Congress he reported "with devout thanksgiving to God, and emotions of joy which no language can express." Church bells rang in Boston, and that evening a jubilee meeting of abolitionists in Music Hall heard Garrison, his voice choked with emotion, declare slavery dead. Phillips was not so certain. The Negro was not yet assured of the ballot, nor was he in any sense guaranteed full civil rights. The Thirteenth Amendment was still to be ratified by the States. Garrison, in his opinion, was far too sanguine.

Garrison and Phillips clashed again at the meeting of the Massachusetts Antislavery Society a few days later. The society, said Phillips, should go on record in favor of

immediate enfranchisement of the Negro. The Negro did
not have the ballot in several Northern states, replied Garrison, and it was clearly unfair to force the issue on the
South until the North itself changed its laws — Connecticut, New Jersey, Pennsylvania, and several Western states
still barred Negroes from the polls. This time Phillips had
the votes. Garrison's resolutions were tabled; Phillips's
passed.

The second encounter was just as decisive. The society's
work, said Garrison, was done. Having brought about the
end of slavery, it might "honorably and gracefully cease
from its specific work." Therefore he moved that the society dissolve. The Phillips faction promptly tabled his
motion again, and to make matters worse, several speakers
politely intimated that since Garrison seemed to have
fallen behind the advance guard of abolitionist thought,
he might well abdicate his presidency to Phillips, who appeared to represent the society's views more accurately.
Garrison very nearly lost his temper. "Neither is he in advance," he said, "nor am I behind; neither does he lead,
nor are the abolitionists led. We stand side by side, shoulder to shoulder, and march in a solid phalanx against the
common foe — God alone being our leader." But he was
wrong. The Massachusetts Antislavery Society no longer
belonged to him.

After the meeting Garrison's spirits were revived by an
invitation from Secretary of War Stanton to attend the
flag-raising ceremonies at Fort Sumter on April 13, the anniversary of its surrender. Thompson, who had arrived in
the United States in 1864, went with him in early April to
witness "the final triumph of Garrisonian abolition." It
was pleasant to be feted, and Garrison enjoyed the trip

thoroughly. After the ceremonies he visited his son in army camp and toured South Carolina and Florida, met everywhere by cheering Negroes who pelted him with flowers and surged after him in crowds to touch his clothes. In Charleston, where a price had once been placed on his head, he spoke to an exultant crowd of Negroes, recalling his long battle for their freedom. "Of one thing I feel sure," he said of Lincoln, "either he has become a Garrisonian Abolitionist or I have become a Lincoln Emancipationist, for I know that we blend, like kindred drops, into one." Four hours after he spoke, Booth shot Lincoln, and when the news of the President's death reached Charleston the next morning Garrison hurried back to New York. It was a sad homecoming, he wrote. "The heavens seemed dark. Nothing was left, for the hour, but God."

The May meeting of the American Antislavery Society in New York was well attended, since everyone knew that the struggle between Garrison and Phillips, begun in Boston, would be carried into the national group. Garrison had no "antislavery boatload" this time, and Phillips had done his organizational work very well. Garrison opened the meeting with a set of resolutions calling for the dissolution of the society, remarking that "it is an anomaly, a solecism, an absurdity, to maintain an antislavery society after slavery is dead." It was time for abolitionists to join the Union as ordinary citizens, to "mingle with the millions of our fellow-countrymen in one common effort to establish justice and liberty throughout the land."

Not so, replied Phillips. The Thirteenth Amendment was not yet ratified, slaves were still legally held in bondage, and the Amendment itself gave freedmen no assurance of full civil rights or of equality. The struggle to give the Negro freedom was only beginning. "I shall never leave the Negro," Phillips cried, "until, so far as God gives me the power, I achieve it!"

The debate lasted two days. Tempers were hot, and in the end Garrison's resolution to dissolve the society lost, 118–48. The nominating committee generously renominated Garrison as the society's president, but he knew it was the end, and after a brief speech of thanks to the faithful forty-eight who had supported him, he made his "affectionate adieu." "My vocation as an abolitionist is ended," he told Oliver Johnson; and ended, too, was his association with the organization he had dominated for a quarter century. Phillips went in as president of the national society, but the bitterness remained. Quincy, May, Gay, Wright, and Johnson left the society with Garrison, and Johnson resigned from the *National Antislavery Standard*. "Half the men I worked with for thirty years," wrote Phillips, "will not speak to me when I meet them in the street."

Garrison went back to the *Liberator*. There were not many subscribers, nor did the paper seem to have much to say. The Radical Republican school of thought, represented by Phillips, Sumner, Stevens, Wade, and the others, went far beyond it, and Garrison had little taste for their wrangle with Andrew Johnson. He took one lecture tour of the West, as far as Quincy, Illinois, chiefly to replenish the *Liberator's* treasury, and announced on his return that he would close its files in December, 1865, rounding out a full thirty-five years of existence. Since it had been founded to battle a system which soon would be extinct by constitutional decree, the *Liberator* had outlived its usefulness —

"Whether we shall retire altogether, or commence anew
. . . we leave it for a Divine Providence to determine."

The last issue of the *Liberator* appeared on December 29, 1865. Garrison read the proofs himself, set the type for the final paragraphs with his own hands, and locked the forms. With his sons George and Frank beside him, he watched the last printing in silence, and then left for a meeting of the New England Freedmen's Association. His final editorial was cheerful. The paper, he said, began without a subscriber and ended without a farthing. He had tried always to conduct it fairly, and although it had excited fierce hostility it had also won the affection of thousands. By a stroke of fate the news of the final ratification of the Thirteenth Amendment by the necessary majority of twenty-seven states arrived in time for the last issue.

Garrison's public life stopped with the *Liberator*. He went to the annual meeting of the Massachusetts society a month later, ran into Phillips again, and quietly dropped his membership after giving Phillips his good wishes. He never attended another abolitionist society meeting in his life. He had sold his Dix Place house in the autumn of 1864, moving to Roxbury, and after the *Liberator* ceased he sat in Roxbury "like a hen plucked of her feathers," reading and clipping newspapers, playing whist, or talking with George Thompson, who rented a house nearby. A fall left him with a shoulder injury, and although his health was fair, he experimented as he had for years with patent medicines and nostrums, complaining of new and unusual illnesses. For several months, from force of habit, he stopped daily at the Massachusetts Antislavery Society offices, where there was nothing for him to do but chat with friends. He visited his daughter (Mrs. Henry Villard) in Washington, talked with Congressmen, and gave a few statements to the papers. Politics had little interest for him and friends persuaded him to go on a short lecture tour. Audiences were enthusiastic, but his shoulder pained him and he gave it up. When the Boston publishing firm of Ticknor and Fields offered him a contract for a history of the abolitionist movement, he accepted with anticipation, moved the *Liberator* files into a rented office, and settled down to work, but, as he told May, he simply did not know where to begin. He worked on the project occasionally for nearly two years before he dropped it.

After more than a year of casting about for something to do, Garrison was gratified to be named as a delegate from the American Freedmen's Union Commission to an International Antislavery Conference in Paris. But that too failed to arouse his enthusiasm. Garrison knew no French, nor did he like France. Discussions among Napoleon III, Bismarck, the Czar, and the King of Prussia were going on at the time, and the massive military reviews in their honor pained his pacifist soul. Since the conference did not begin until August, he crossed to England.

Garrison's British reputation, always bright, shone at its brightest in 1867. More than any man except Lincoln, he was regarded by British liberals as the guiding genius of American emancipation. On June 20, 1867, a ceremonial "public breakfast" was held in his honor at St. James's Hall, with all three hundred tickets sold out. John Bright presided, and for two hours Garrison listened to the plaudits of the British antislavery leaders — Earl Russell, John

Stuart Mill, the Duke of Argyll — while Buxton, Huxley, Lord Houghton, and others applauded him. When Garrison rose to reply, the hall rose with him in respect. Obviously affected by emotion, he spoke quietly and briefly. "I have simply tried," he said, "to maintain the integrity of my soul before God, and to do my duty. I have refused to go with the multitude to do evil. I have endeavored to save my country from ruin. . . . But now, God be praised, she is free — free to advance the cause of liberty throughout the world." Praise and good wishes followed him through the rest of his tour. Manchester invited him to speak, and so did Newcastle, Edinburgh, and Glasgow. Everywhere the crowds were enthusiastic and his reception tumultuous. It "made his heart full," he said, and he regretted that he had to return to Paris.

The International Antislavery Conference was a disappointment. He could understand only a few speeches and the discussion was lukewarm, since the law of the Second Empire forbade the presentation of views not previously approved by the Security Police. Garrison himself spoke but once, giving a short history of the American abolitionist movement and passing words of encouragement to the delegates from Spain, Portugal, and Brazil, where slavery still existed. He was also exhausted from his British tour, and glad to leave with his children for a trip through Switzerland, Germany, Belgium, and a short visit to England again.

When he returned to the United States in October, 1867, his friends had a surprise for him. Knowing that his finances were always precarious, Henry Bowditch of Boston had formed a committee in 1866 to raise a "National Testimonial" fund. Ex-Governor Andrew of Massachusetts accepted the chairmanship and wrote its appeal for donations. Almost all the members of the Massachusetts legislature appended their names, all of the Massachusetts Congressmen, both Senators, the Chief Justice of the United States Supreme Court, leading citizens in every major city, and such literary figures as Emerson, Whittier, Longfellow, Lowell, and Bryant — some six hundred signers in all. The goal was $50,000, and by the time of Garrison's return the committee had collected $31,000, exclusive of £300 sent from England. In the spring of 1868 they gave him the money. "I accept it," he replied, "not as relating to any other question than that of slavery, not as an approval of all my methods of action and modes of expression . . . but exactly for what it is intended to sanction and commend, to wit — the cause of universal freedom and an unswerving advocacy of that cause, at whatever peril." That so many thousands would contribute to the comfort of a man once so obscure that the Mayor of Boston could not find him, a man on whose head a state had once placed a price, and one whose language had for three decades stirred up violence and fear, seemed to Garrison the final accolade of rightness.

Phillips led the Massachusetts and the American Antislavery Societies down his own road into radical politics while they both languished. His influence as a speaker for the radical cause was considerable; Andrew Johnson believed him at least as dangerous an opponent as Stevens or Sumner. But Phillips went deeper and deeper into third-party politics, into the Prohibition and Labor-Reform Parties, and took up the unpopular cause of labor, arguing for unions as brilliantly as he ever did for abolition.

He hoped to capture the Massachusetts Republican Party, joining laborite, prohibitionist, and ex-abolitionist into one big coalition.

His alliance with unsavory General Ben Butler was more than his friends could stand. Emerson, Sumner, and Henry Wilson broke with him, while Phillips took up greenbackism and the Irish question, scattering his genius among ephemeral causes. His wife Ann, ill for years, burdened his thoughts; years of open-handed spending reduced his once comfortable fortune to a pittance. Friends noted he wore darned gloves and detected an air of repressed desperation in his manner, a bitterness and melancholy foreign to his nature. The truth was that when abolitionism died, much of Phillips's crusading energy died with it. Neither labor, nor tariff, nor Ireland, nor greenbacks seemed quite worthy of his tempered steel, and try as he would the old eloquence was gone. Unlike Garrison, Phillips could never retire, for there was still too much to be done before life ended.

While Phillips chased the success that always eluded him, Garrison rested at Roxbury. He favored various current reforms, lent his name to several of them, but without the enthusiasm of thirty years before. "Our danger lies in sensual indulgence," he told W. G. H. Smart, "in a licentious perversion of liberty, in the prevalence of intemperance, and in whatever tends to the demoralization of the people" — inward reform, perhaps, was more important than organized crusades. Phillips's course he neither approved nor understood. He had one more brush with Phillips, though the two had agreed to declare peace and had begun to exchange letters. Francis Jackson's will had left a fund for furthering the antislavery cause, to be administered by a board of trustees on which both Garrison and Phillips served. Phillips proposed that the money be used to pay off the debts of the *National Antislavery Standard,* which still struggled on under the sponsorship of the dying national society; Garrison contended it should be used to establish schools for Negroes. Phillips won, but Garrison took the matter to court and got the board's decision reversed. It mattered little, since the *Standard,* the schools and the society collapsed in two years. Garrison did not even bother to attend the society's last meeting.

Oliver Johnson, associate editor of the New York *Independent,* a leading religious newspaper, offered Garrison a post as a regular paid contributor in 1868. Garrison accepted, glad of a way to spend his time, and contributed more than a hundred articles over the next seven years. They were, as one correspondent said, "specimens of fine English," but little more. Only infrequently did they flash with the Old Testament fire of the early Garrison. His interests were still wide, his mind alert, and his shibboleth was still reform — women's rights, temperance, nonresistance, a universal language, theology, free trade, and so on — but the nation was not interested in reform and Garrison had no real understanding of the issues of the times. "It is enough for me," he said, "that every yoke is broken, and every bondman set free." He attacked the Ku-Klux Klan, the Red Shirts, and other terroristic groups, and supported Grant through both terms, parting company with his friend Sumner on the Liberal Republican movement of 1872. Yet politics held little attraction for him. He had an opportunity to replace Sumner in the Senate after the latter's death in 1874, but declined the appointment on the ground that he could never take an oath to support a

Constitution that contained war clauses. The old belief that moral and political action did not mix prompted him to censure Phillips for accepting the Prohibition Party's nomination for governor in 1870 and to refuse its nomination for President in 1876. He agreed to serve as associate editor of the *Woman's Journal,* and helped to found the American Woman Suffrage Association. He was not willing, however, to throw himself into the women's rights battle as of old. To Susan B. Anthony, who asked his help in circulating a petition to Congress, he replied that the whole movement was "premature," and that "even as a matter of agitation I do not think it would pay."

Helen Eliza Garrison died in January, 1876, and Garrison was too ill to attend her funeral. Phillips spoke at the services, for the years had healed the old wounds. Afterwards the house at Roxbury was full of loneliness for Garrison. In the spring of 1877 his children persuaded him to take a trip abroad. His friend Edmund Quincy died the day he embarked, but once aboard ship he threw off his depression and enjoyed himself. Not many of the old workers were left in England; there were a few receptions, a few breakfasts, and many visitors. He spoke to a meeting of the National Women's Suffrage Association, visited Westminster Abbey, and simply toured as a sightseer. In July he spent a week with George Thompson, who was a shattered wreck of a man, his throat paralyzed and his legs crippled, with less than a year to live. When the time came to part, the two old men embraced in tears, knowing they would never see each other again.

Life in Roxbury was quiet. Garrison spent much of his time in meditation, rousing himself now and then to write to friends. On October 13, 1878, the sixtieth anniversary of his apprenticeship as a printer, he traveled to Newburyport to set a stick of type in the old *Herald* offices. He set up three of his own sonnets without an error and afterwards journeyed to Boston to be the dinner guest of the Franklin Club, a group of printers. On the forty-third anniversary of the Boston riots, Phillips, James Buffum, Alcott, and a few others held an informal memorial meeting for him at the Women's Club, the last gathering he ever attended.

Garrison's health failed rapidly. By late 1878 he found it difficult to leave his house. In April, 1879, his children persuaded him to move to New York City to live with his daughter, and within a few days of his arrival he suffered a severe kidney infection. Through May he lived mostly in a coma. On May 23 his doctor, seeing the old man stir, asked him, "What do you want, Mr. Garrison?" The reply came clearly, "To finish it up!" — the last challenge of some long-ago battle. The next day, shortly before midnight, he died.

On May 28, 1879, William Lloyd Garrison was buried in the family plot at Roxbury. The Governor of Massachusetts proclaimed an official day of mourning, and at Negro churches throughout the nation black men and women gathered in silent prayer for his soul. Since Garrison had often expressed his belief that death was not an occasion for sadness, the shutters of the Roxbury house were thrown open and the pulpit was decorated with flowers. Samuel May, junior, conducted the services, Lucy Stone and old Theodore Weld spoke, and a Negro quartet sang Garrison's favorite hymns. Whittier, who came over from Amesbury, was too deeply moved to read the poem he had written for the occasion, and May read it for him. Oliver Johnson was there, Wendell Phillips, Lewis Hayden, Samuel Sewall — all the survivors of the Massachusetts movement. The unquiet spirit of William Lloyd Garrison rested at last in the quiet earth.

Epilogue

To THOSE AROUND HIM, Garrison was very nearly
a deity, already safely immortal. To those who opposed
him, he was an archrebel, a wrecker, a man incapable of
cooperation or moderation. The human Garrison was
known only to his family and a few close friends. Five feet
nine, compactly built, he had hazel eyes, large teeth, a
ruddy complexion, and brown hair before baldness came
in his twenties. He suffered from what his generation
called "weak lungs" and from headaches, probably caused
by eyestrain and overwork, but his physical condition was
usually better than he assumed it to be. His letters referred constantly to minor illnesses, often fancied, and he
was an easy mark for nostrums and quack remedies —
much to the amusement of his friends, who knew they usually contained a high percentage of alcohol. He had his
normal share of foibles. He disliked cats, beards, and steel
pens. He would not attend dinners at which cigars were
passed, and he was always ready to exhort abolitionist
friends to "stop clouding their brains" with smoke. He
thought most of the art in the Louvre rubbish, liked to
play checkers, whist, and quoits, and liked to sing hymns
with his family. He hated ostentation and display, believ-

ing with the Quakers that both were vulgar and dangerous to morals. He committed reams of oratory and bad poetry to memory and often declaimed it, with gestures, for his own enjoyment. The prevailing sentimental interest in nature he would have none of; he was a city man who found no message in flowers or morals in vistas, and who preferred the excitement and rustle of crowds.

There was little lightness or humor in Garrison. He was a deadly serious man. In thirty-five volumes of the *Liberator* it is difficult to find a joke. His letters to his wife had a serious, oratorical quality, as if he were writing for publication, and his platform style, like his editorials, was tense and purposeful. He wrote a serviceable, energetic prose, rough at the edges but muscular and direct, filled with echoes of the King James Version and Baptist sermons. His speeches were sober and serious. He was never a master of the golden phrase or the witty twist, as Phillips was, though he was capable of an occasional flash of imagery or dramatic turn of language. Writing or speaking or living, he was always the agitator, the editorializer, the crusader, searching for the word that convinced or the phrase that incited.

Garrison's mind worked on two levels, the moral and the practical. On the one, his approach to issues was determined by principle; on the other, by tactics and strategy. The level of his argument fluctuated, as it did during the Civil War when he scourged Lincoln on principles, yet pleaded the value of expediency. Fundamentally, his approach to things was simple and consistent. He judged everything by two standards of moral right — natural law as expressed in the Declaration of Independence, and

Christian ethic as expressed in the Bible. To him these
were essentially one, emanating from the same divine
source. Any idea or institution which violated either, in
part or whole, therefore was wrong. The final judgment
rested with individual conscience, the roots of which lay in
God. A world of conscience so rooted was Garrison's "kingdom to be established on earth," in which the individual's own soul became the arbiter of action and the judge of
institutions — a kingdom in which men voluntarily ceased
to sin, established justice, and worshiped God in a "magis-
tracy of holiness and love."

The central fact of Garrison's life was his religious
faith. The Bible was the only book he ever really read,
and his abolitionism itself sprang directly from his belief
that slavery violated God's law. "It was not on account of
your complexion or race, as a people, that I espoused your
cause," he told a Negro meeting in Charleston in 1865,
"but because you were the children of a common Father,
created in the same divine image, having the same inalienable rights. . . ." Despite the charge of "infidelity"
that followed him wherever he went, he was a rigidly religious man. The bland neutrality of nineteenth-century
Unitarianism was not for him. The finespun speculations
of New England transcendentalism lay beyond his capacity; even Lyman Beecher's brand of modified Calvinism
was too soft. Instead he returned to an earlier, rigorous
faith, straight from his Bible. In 1842, stung to exaspera-
tion by accusations of "infidelity," he published his creed
in the *Liberator*:

I believe that, in Jesus Christ, the believer is dead unto sin,
and alive with God — that whosoever is born of God over-
cometh the world — that Christ is the end of the law for

righteousness, to everyone who believeth. . . . I believe that priestcraft, and sectarianism, and slavery, and war, and everything that defileth or maketh a lie, are of the devil, and destined to an eternal overthrow.

The language was the language of the Old Testament, the spirit that of third-century Christianity. He had the zeal and fanaticism of a Biblical prophet, combined with apostolic dedication. His religion, he said, was "that of the Jewish religionists of eighteen centuries ago," and his God a Hebraic God who spoke directly to his conscience. Him and only Him would Garrison obey and call Master.

From this Godbased individualism flowed Garrison's revolt against manmade authority — abolition, disunion, pacifism, perfectionism, women's rights, and "infidelity." "Individual, personal effort" — he wrote —

is the true foundation of all real prosperity in the social state, and all excellence of character. No form of Society can be devised which will release the individual from personal responsibility. . . . It would be the greatest curse that could be inflicted upon him.

Garrison thus did not belong in an age of conciliation and compromise, nor was he fitted for what his era called "the principle of association." He liked, he said, "causes which, being righteous, are unpopular, and struggling, in God's name, against wind and tide." With God and conscience on his side, turmoil was his natural element. "Hisses," he once said, "are music to my ears." Organizations strait-jacketed him; he accepted them only as utensils for his own use. Temperamentally he was a no-government man and his aversion to cooperation was as ingrained as Thoreau's.

Garrison was a true revolutionary individualist who accepted nothing beyond himself, no tradition or institution whose existence violated his own inner, higher law. There was something of the eighteenth-century rebel in him, and more of the seventeenth-century Puritan's self-righteous independence. Emerson, too, preached the sufficiency of self and the integrity of self-reliance as God-reliance, but Garrison's deity was no transcendental Oversoul. His was a stern, inflexible God of wrath and justice, his individualism a flinty, arrogant self-faith. Emerson's individualism was ascetic and intellectual; Garrison's was visceral, emotional. He could never have taken to the woods as Thoreau did. He was a social being, tied to humanity and incapable of acting without it. As Emerson shrewdly remarked, Garrison "would find nohing to do in a lonely world, or a world with half-a-dozen inhabitants."

Acting from his own driving religious faith and within the terms of his society, Garrison had every reason to be what he was — the Reformer Incarnate. He conceived himself to be the tool of God, his followers "soldiers of God" with "loins girt about with truth" and "feet shod with the preparation of the Gospel of peace." His aim was nothing less than "the emancipation of our whole race from the dominion of man, from the thraldom of self, from the government of brute force, from the bondage of sin." This was the New Jerusalem, the kingdom of God awaited by the Hebrew prophets. The complete freedom of man was to him the whole purpose of life, and he lived with single-minded devotion to it.

Those who accused Garrison of deserting the main battle of abolition for minor skirmishes failed to recognize that to Garrison no reform, however close to the lunatic fringe, was unrelated to the larger purpose. He was always, as he said late in life, interested in nothing less than "the redemption of the human race." If the human race needed redemption from slavery on the one hand and cigar-smoking on the other, there was no reason to neglect one crusade for another if both could proceed at once. Bronson Alcott, of all Garrison's contemporaries, understood the grand sweep of his design and saw what the others missed. He was, Alcott wrote in his journal, wholly "intent on the melioration of human woes and the eradication of human evils." Nothing else could satisfy him. Garrison was no intellectual, but a man of action. He never liked to speculate, and he had no reverence for reflection. Emerson once said that Garrison "neighed like a horse" when they discussed ideas. Unlike Emerson, Garrison never tried to search hard for truth, because he had it.

The moral self-righteousness that lay beneath Garrison's crusade for the kingdom of God on earth was difficult to accept. There was no vacillation in him, no gray in his thinking, only right and wrong, deep black and pure white. There could be no compromise with sin and only Garrison could define sin. To disagree with him was to disagree with Right personified. In the last analysis his final court of appeal was conscience, not mind. Moral judgment was his first and last line of defense, and for this reason it was almost impossible to persuade him he was wrong. Founded on God and conscience, his stand was impregnable.

This absolute self-confidence was one reason his band followed him with worship this side of idolatry. Garrison had no hesitations, no questionings, no doubts, and inspired the same self-assurance in others. His sincerity and

courage attracted men so widely different as the gentle
May, the urbane Phillips, the wildly unstable Foster, and
the unpredictable Wright. Some of his twists and turns
made his most ardent supporters swallow hard, but Garrison to the end of his life believed himself perfectly consistent and unassailably right. His enemies always respected
his obstinate sincerity. They sometimes thought he was
wrong, or arrogant, or unreasonable — but never insin-
cere. He was capable of absolute identification with a
principle. If he believed in an idea he would die for it,
though it be ill-advised, wrong, or downright foolish. This
monolithic self-confidence drew men to him.

Garrison's faith in himself made him unconsciously dictatorial. He genuinely considered himself a modest man,
refusing personal praise and credit. Yet he constantly
sought it with a real inward hunger. His personality felt
a deep need for recognition. He never aspired to political
office, though certainly after 1861 he could have had it.
He paid little attention to money, security, or possessions.
He simply neglected to write his memoirs when he could
have made thousands, and the financial status of the *Liberator* was always more important to him than his own. But
he was sure from the first that he was a man for the ages,
and he felt compelled to keep reminding himself and
others of the fact. His remarks in the *Liberator,* less than a
year after its inception, were not those of a humble, self-
effacing young man: "The present generation cannot appreciate the purity of my motives or the value of my exer-
tions. I look to posterity for a good reputation. The
unborn offspring of those who are now living will reverse
the condemnatory decision of my contemporaries." Again,
a few months later, he turned to a companion on leaving a

meeting to remark, "You may someday write my biography."

Garrison was not averse to comparing himself to the Apostles, though he obviously possessed little of their patience and forbearance. He rarely forgot or forgave those who differed with him, and occasionally he took more credit where less was due without the slightest embarrassment. He had not, as Alcott put it trenchantly, "won those self-victories which lead to the superior powers of those who have won themselves." Significantly, Garrison had only a limited circle of close friends — "God's choreboy" Samuel May, Johnson, Quincy, and, closest of all, George Thompson, a man much like himself. Garrison lived in terms of his future epitaph, and carried his own Westminster Abbey about with him.

William Lloyd Garrison's place in history was hotly debated in his own time. His admirers made him a greater man than he was, and his opponents gave him less praise than he deserved. According to Wendell Phillips, Garrison "began, inspired, and largely controlled" the entire abolition movement from beginning to end. Another idolator called him "lawgiver at Washington, inspirer of Presidential policy, and framer of the greatest war of modern times." But William Birney regarded Garrisonism as "the most utter abortion known in the history of this country," and Henry Ward Beecher characterized him as "no more than a blister" on the antislavery movement. Neither the Tappans, nor Birney, nor Lundy, nor Weld, nor any of the pioneer abolitionists beyond New England thought of Garrison as more than an intractable, disturbing though sincere and devoted co-worker whose misguided zeal sometimes brought more harm than good to the cause.

The Garrison legend was partly the result of reams of uncritical praise poured out by Garrisonians — May, Johnson, Phillips, and others — in contrast to the comparative silence of those who opposed him. More than a little of Garrison's own conviction of immortality rubbed off on his followers. "Garrison has an army of men to write him up," said E. L. Pierce in 1892, "and his writers are unscrupulous." Those who admired Garrison gloried in praising him; those who opposed him charitably kept quiet.

It is only fair to grant Garrison pre-eminence in the first decade of abolition agitation. He personified its aggressive phase, publicized it for better or worse, and drove its issues deep into the national conscience. But he did not begin abolitionism, nor did he organize it. Weld and the Westerners, and the Tappans and the New Yorkers, deserve a large share of the credit; had Garrison never existed things might have been much the same. The movement, set in motion by others, was carried to its conclusion by methods he could not accept and ideas he could not understand. Abolition passed through him, not from him.

Yet Garrison was a person of real historical importance, for he was a symbol to his generation of the moral and ideological conflict that took its final shape in the Civil War. To the South, he represented all that was baleful and dangerous. Whatever his insistence on pacific intentions, he stirred up violent resentments and his appeals reached the passions rather than the consciences of slaveholders. His principle of "moral agitation" against slavery created only agitation. The proslavery forces, already consolidating, could concentrate all their fear and anger on him. If the approaching conflict was irrepressible, Garrison was at least a factor in convincing the South that it was so. By proslavery logic, Garrison led to John Brown; Brown led to Lincoln; Garrison, Brown, and Lincoln together led to an intolerable conclusion. It was easier for the South to argue from personalities than from principles, and Garrison was a personality no Southerner could overlook. By very little effort of his own he became a bogeyman to the South and a personification to it of things to come.

To the North, Garrison was a goad, a prick to the conscience, a symbol of the moral problem of slavery that remained unsolved despite compromises, conciliations, and tacit agreements to disregard it. Slavery, no matter how it was explained or rationalized, *did* exist; the fact of its existence *was* an anomaly in a nation dedicated to life, liberty, and the individual's right to pursue happiness. Garrison, more than any other one person, shattered the "conspiracy of silence." One might decry his invective, censure his methods, or deny his appeal to disorder; one could never shut out his clamor. To disagree with Garrison men had to face up to the problem, rethink their beliefs, examine their own consciences. When men did this, slavery was doomed. Garrison contributed relatively little to the philosophy of abolitionism. He had only a single thought — that "slavery was a crime, a damning crime" — but he made other men think, though he sometimes muddled their thinking. Economic and political events that Garrison neither knew nor cared about made slavery a national issue and precipitated the war. But it had its moral causes too, which Garrison's career aptly symbolized to the victorious North.

A Note on the Sources [1]

THE MOST COMPREHENSIVE STUDY of William Lloyd Garrison is *William Lloyd Garrison, 1805–1879: The Story of his Life told by his Children* (New York, 1885–1889), by Wendell Phillips Garrison and Francis Jackson Garrison. The Garrisons' biography of their father, in four thick volumes, provides a month-to-month account of his life, reprints the majority of his letters and speeches, and contains large amounts of tangential materials. While William Birney's charge against the Garrison children's biography is perhaps too harsh — that it is "a legal brief filed for posterity in behalf of William Lloyd Garrison" — its editors undoubtedly wrote from an understandable bias, glossed over many incidents, and occasionally suppressed useful evidence. Nevertheless, the volumes are still "the quarry," as Fanny Garrison Villard called it, "from which all subsequent lives of William Lloyd Garrison have necessarily been written."

Contemporary accounts of Garrison written by his co-workers are overwhelmingly adulatory. Samuel J. May's *Recollections of the Anti-Slavery Conflict* (Boston, 1869) is strongly prejudiced; it is, however, a valuable account of New England abolitionism and of Garrison's early antislavery activity. Oliver Johnson's biography, *William Lloyd Garrison and his Times* (Boston, 1881), written by Garrison's long-time editorial assist-

[1] The writer expresses his thanks to Frank Hodgins and Milton Stern for assistance in preparing this note.

ant, is similarly biased in his favor, but is also an excellent source of information. Goldwin Smith's *The Moral Crusader, William Lloyd Garrison* (New York, 1892) rehashes parts of the Garrison sons' larger study, while Lindsay Swift, *William Lloyd Garrison* (Philadelphia, 1911), and Archibald Grimké, *William Lloyd Garrison, The Abolitionist* (New York, 1892), contribute little. Fred Douglass's *Life and Times* (Hartford, 1882) throws some interesting sidelights on Garrison and the New England group.

Fanny Garrison Villard's *William Lloyd Garrison on Non-Resistance* (New York, 1924) is a brief study of Garrison's pacifism by his daughter. Harriet Martineau's *The Martyr Age of the United States of America* (Newcastle, 1840) is an overview of early abolitionism, with Garrison occupying a prominent place, by an intelligent Englishwoman. Henry Wilson's *History of the Rise and Fall of the Slave Power in America* (Boston, 1872) is an exhaustive but untrustworthy account of the entire antislavery conflict. William Birney's study of his father, *James G. Birney and His Times* (New York, 1890), presents the anti-Garrisonian point of view with some heat and serves as a corrective to May and Johnson. Birney's and Weld's judgments of Garrison and of his place in the antislavery movement may be gathered from their references to him, available in D. L. Dumond's edition of *The Letters of James G. Birney* (New York, 1938), and in Dumond and G. H. Barnes, *The Letters of Theodore Weld, Angelina Grimké Weld, and Sarah Grimké* (New York, 1934).

Of the several studies of Garrison made since the turn of the century, two deserve mention. John Jay Chapman's *William Lloyd Garrison* (New York, 1913), while not a detailed biography, is a perceptive analysis of Garrison's mind and personality. Ralph Korngold's *Two Friends of Man* (Boston, 1950), a double biography of Garrison and Phillips, is by far the best of the recent studies of Garrison and abolitionism.

Among older studies of abolition and of Garrison's place in it, A. B. Hart's *Slavery and Abolition* (New York, 1906) and Jesse Macy, *The Anti-Slavery Crusade* (New Haven, 1919), still have validity. A. Y. Lloyd, *The Slavery Controversy, 1831–1860*

(Chapel Hill, 1939), is a good specialized study of the pro-slavery and antislavery argument, though unsympathetic to Garrison and the abolitionists. The best treatment of Garrison as a journalist is that contained in Joseph A. DelPorto, *A Study of American Antislavery Journals* (unpublished dissertation, Michigan State College, 1953). Alice Felt Tyler's *Freedom's Ferment* (Minneapolis, 1944) gives a comprehensive and readable account of the burgeoning of nineteenth-century reform, abolition included, and R. B. Nye, *Fettered Freedom* (East Lansing, 1949), traces the relationships between abolition and civil liberties before 1861. Merle Curti's *The American Peace Crusade, 1815–1860* (Durham, 1929) provides a good account of nineteenth-century pacifism and Garrison's place in the peace movement. The most important recent study of abolitionism is Gilbert H. Barnes's *The Antislavery Impulse 1830–1844* (New York, 1933), a plausible though perhaps over-balanced re-evaluation of Garrison and Weld as antislavery leaders that challenges the long-accepted view of Garrison's pre-eminence in abolitionist history.

Index

Date Due